The

Art of

STONE SKIPPING
AND OTHER FUN
OLD-TIME GAMES

imagine!
Publishing

The Art of

STONE SKIPPING
AND OTHER FUN
OLD-TIME GAMES

Stoopball, Jacks, String Games, Coin Flipping, Line Baseball, Jump Rope, and More

J. J. Ferrer

illustrated by Todd Dakins

imagine!
Publishing

An Imagine Book
Published by Charlesbridge Publishing, Inc.
85 Main Street, Watertown, MA 02472
(617) 926-0329
www.charlesbridge.com

Text copyright © 2012 by J. J. Ferrer.
Illustrations copyright © 2012 by Charlesbridge Publishing, Inc.
Interior and cover design by Melissa Gerber.
Rock Paper Scissors Lizard Spock image used with the permission of Sam Kass and Karen Bryla.
All rights reserved, including the right of reproduction in whole or in part in any form. Charlesbridge and colophon are registered trademarks of Charlesbridge Publishing, Inc.
Printed in China in September 2012.

Library of Congress Cataloging-in-Publication Data

Ferrer, J. J.
  The art of stone skipping and other fun old-time games : stoopball,
jacks, string games, coin flipping, line baseball, jump rope, and more/ by J.J.
Ferrer ; illustrated by Todd Dakins.
      p. cm.
  Includes bibliographical references and index.
  ISBN 978-1-936140-74-9 (alk. paper)
  1. Games. I. Title.
  GV1203.F368 2012
  790.1'922--dc23
                                    2012015052

ISBN 978-1-936140-74-9
2 4 6 8 10 9 7 5 3 1

For information about custom editions, special sales,
premium and corporate purchases, please contact
Charlesbridge Publishing at specialsales@charlesbridge.com

TABLE OF CONTENTS

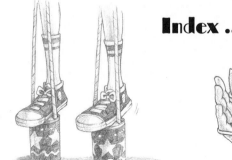

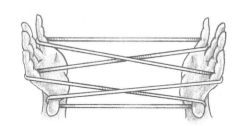

To all those moms who kept the welcome mat out and the Kool-Aid coming: Thanks for a wonderful childhood. May there be many more like you for generations to come. —J.J.F.

INTRODUCTION

Archaeologists have found enough carved wooden game pieces, leather balls, and clay dice to prove that playing games has been a part of every civilization since the beginning of time. Even in cultures where children were expected to work alongside adults rather than play freely, kids have always turned to games for fun and recreation, whether competing against friends or simply challenging themselves. We know from artifacts that children were playing board games in China as early as 2000 BC, marbles in Greece by 400 BC, and ball in Egypt by 2 BC.

Balls may well be the oldest of all toys. Early ones were made from strips of leather, cloth, or papyrus sewn together, then stuffed with hair, feathers, or straw. Balls were also made from animal skulls and bladders and, in some cultures, even the heads of enemies! Simple games of catch, in which one child threw a ball up in the air and caught it or two children tossed a ball back and forth to each other, probably happened as soon as Cain and Abel were old enough to walk. But history tells us that the first "organized" ball games happened in Mexico nearly four thousand years ago, with teams of two to six players trying to get a really heavy ball across their opponents' goal line. Ball games weren't always just for fun, though: Sometimes they had religious purposes, and sometimes the losing team lost their heads as well as the game!

Card games have also been around a really long time; they date back to the seventh century. Archaeological evidence of cards made from animal skins, ivory, leaves, leather, and woodblock prints has been found in China, India, Korea, and the Middle East. While today's cards are typically rectangular and made of paper or plastic, with four suits, fifty-two cards, and two jokers in the deck, earlier cards were often round, with three suits and a deck of only thirty. No one knows exactly how kings, queens, jacks (a servant boy), and jokers became the poster people for cards, but it's probably because card playing was a favorite game of the court—and you know those royal egos. At one point, some monarchy even declared that card playing was off-limits to commoners! But thankfully that changed, and today playing cards is a favorite hobby for people of all ages—even those of us without kingdoms and crowns.

Most games that we play today have their roots in early diversions that were passed down from one generation to the next. Fun as they were, the games were often a way to teach skills and strategies critical for survival—everything from patience and ingenuity to speed and accuracy. Today, these time-honored games still help children learn new skills, discover unknown strengths, and build peer relations—which translates directly into solving problems, creating solutions, and becoming a good team player.

The real purpose of games, though, is to guarantee children a good time—by themselves, with a buddy, with their class, with Grandpa, or maybe even with the family pet. This book contains games that have been vetted by millions of boys and girls, many over thousands of years. They require little equipment and no batteries or electricity, the rules are simple, and the variations are endless.

Enjoy.

BALL GAMES

Ace-Queen-King

(also called Chinese Handball, Down the River, Kings, and Slug)

WHO: 2 or more players

WHAT YOU NEED: a small rubber ball, any paved surface that abuts a wall (ideal situation is a sidewalk with marked squares; you can also use tape or chalk to create a box for each player)

OBJECT: Be the last player to get 11 points.

Players stand in a line parallel to the wall, each in a defined square. Play moves from left to right. The first player, the Ace, bounces the ball off the ground so that it hits the wall and bounces into the square of the player on his right (the King). The King then rebounds the ball onto the sidewalk, off the wall, and into the square of the third player (the Queen). Play continues down the line until it reaches the last player, then play reverses back up the line from right to left. Anyone who misses a ball gets a point and moves to the end of the line, with everyone else moving one space to the left. If the Ace misses a shot, he goes to the end of the line, but does not get a penalty point. As each player reaches 11 points, she must stand in front of the others, bend over, and let each player toss a ball at her backside. This is called Butts Up. The last person to reach 11 points is the winner.

Additional Rules

1. Players can only hit the ball with the palms of their hands.

2. A player must bounce the ball on the ground once before it hits the wall.

3. If a player misses the ball on the rebound or hits it out of bounds, he gets a penalty point and must move to the end of the line.

4. If someone (a fellow player, spectator, passerby) gets in the way when a player is trying to hit the ball, the player can call "Interference!" and start again. If a player deliberately tries to prevent the ball from hitting the wall, however, that player is out of the game.

Variations

• Let whichever player is closest to the ball return it.

• Play to 21 points (or any number you'd like) instead of 11.

Trick Shots

• Behind the Back Shot: Before or after the ball hits the ground, the player hits it behind her back.

• Cobble Smash Shot (also called a Bomb Shot or Shotgun Shot): Player hits the ball with a closed fist instead of his palm.

• Drop Shot: Hitter makes a fist, leans low to the ground, and smacks the ball hard so that it barely bounces and then hits the wall in such a way that a return bounce is impossible.

• Through the Legs Shot (also called a Double and Under Shot): Player lets the ball bounce twice, then hits it so that it goes between her legs.

• Slice Shot: Player hits the ball, hard and downward, with a flat palm. This causes the ball to go down fast, but have a slow return.

• Wormburner Shot: Player hits the ball so it stays low to the ground, then hits the wall at such an angle that it spins, theoretically "burning" the worms in the ground.

Fun Facts: From the 1950s through the 1970s, you could find kids playing Ace-Queen-King or one of its many variations all over the world, especially in urban areas such as New York City.

Boxball
(also called Slap Ball or Punchball)

WHO: 2 players

WHAT YOU NEED: a small rubber ball, sidewalk (if there are no squares on the sidewalk, you'll need tape or chalk to mark them)

OBJECT: Be the first player to get 21 points.

This is a fun and simple game for two players. Think of it as tennis with hands instead of rackets, and on a much smaller court!

Decide who goes first and create three "boxes," or squares, one for each player with one in between. The server throws the ball in the air (or bounces it up) and, using the open palm of his dominant hand, slaps the ball into his opponent's box. With the open palm of her dominant hand, the opponent slaps it back to the server's box after one bounce, or on the fly. Play continues, with the ball slapped back and forth between boxes, until someone fails to return a shot or bounces the ball outside the opponent's box. A point goes to the player who did not miss the shot or bounce out of bounds. The first player to reach 21 points is the winner.

Variations

- Play to 11 (or any number you'd like) instead of 21.

- Use either hand instead of just one, a fist instead of your palm (this is Punchball), or the back of your hand as well as your palm.

- Slap the ball back and forth and try to keep it in the air instead of letting it hit the ground.

- Play more like baseball, with single pitches. If the catcher catches the ball without it bouncing, he gets a point. If the pitcher lands the ball in the catcher's box and it bounces once, the pitcher gets the point. If the pitcher fails to get the ball in the box, he's out and it's the catcher's turn to pitch.

Call Ball

WHO: 3 or more players

WHAT YOU NEED: a bouncing ball such as a tennis ball, room to run

OBJECT: Catch the ball.

Each player chooses a number between one and however many players you have, a day of the week, or a color. The first player bounces the ball as high into the air as possible and calls out a number/day/color. As soon as he calls out, everyone except the player whose number/day/color was called runs away. The player who was called tries to catch the ball before it hits the ground. If he does, then he gets to bounce the ball and call the next play. Play continues until someone fails to catch the ball. When a called player fails to catch the ball, whoever bounced the ball last gets to bounce and call again.

Variations

• Instead of numbers, days of the week, or colors, players can use the names of sports teams, types of dogs, types of cars, letters of the alphabet, or any other category.

• When the called player fails to catch the ball, he loses one point, then yells "Stop!" Everyone else freezes. The called player retrieves the ball, then throws it at any player except the one who originally bounced the ball. If the ball doesn't hit anyone, that player loses another point and the ball goes back to the original bouncer. If the ball does hit someone, that player loses a point, but gets to bounce the ball and call out the next player.

Fun Facts: When Charles Goodyear designed and built the first vulcanized rubber ball in 1855, "play ball!" took on a whole new meaning. Then paved roads and school yards added a whole new dimension to games that had already made these simple orbs an integral part of everyone's childhood.

Catch

WHO: 1 or more players

WHAT YOU NEED: a baseball or softball, a ball glove for each person

OBJECT: Catch the ball.

One person throws the ball and catches it. With two people, throw the ball back and forth. With more than two, each person throws the ball to the next person until everyone's had a chance to catch it, then you repeat the sequence.

Tips

- Put your glove on the hand you do *not* throw with. Line up the glove and your body with the ball, placing the pocket of the glove toward the ball.

- If the ball is coming at about waist level, turn the fingers of your glove in line with your throwing shoulder and hold your throwing hand beside or behind the glove.

- If the ball is high, extend your arm, point your glove fingers toward the sky—with your palm facing the ball—and keep your elbow slightly bent and close to your body.

- If the ball is low, turn the fingers of the glove down and hold it in front of you palm-out, between your legs, with your throwing hand beside or behind the glove. Bend your knees and be ready to scoop the ball up as soon as it gets to you.

- Bending your elbows slightly helps absorb the impact when the ball hits your glove and will help keep it from bouncing out of the glove.

- Squeeze your glove tight when the ball lands in it so it can't roll out.

Variations

- Flies and grounders: Alternate between throwing fly balls and ground balls, making the catcher try to guess what you're going to throw. Two points for catching flies, one point for catching grounders. If the pitcher throws something only a crow could catch, catchers can ask for a redo! Game is over when you reach a predetermined number of points.

- Designate a specific pitching area, such as at the waist or at the knees, and give points if the pitcher's balls land where they're supposed to.

Catch a Fly and You're Up

WHO: 3 or more players

WHAT YOU NEED: a baseball or softball, a bat, gloves for fielders

OBJECT: Catch the ball and you get to bat.

- -

Pitcher throws a ball, batter hits it, and whoever catches it is up to bat.

Variations

- -

- If you don't have a bat or a baseball, any small ball will do. Just have someone pitch the ball, and whoever catches it gets to pitch next.

- Let each batter hit five times. Whichever fielder catches the most balls gets to bat next.

Fun Facts: Catch a Fly and You're Up was a favorite of kids all over America in the 1950s. Many legendary baseball players have fond memories of honing their skills by playing Catch a Fly for hours on end.

Comet Ball

WHO: 3 or more players

WHAT YOU NEED: a sock, a tennis ball or small rubber ball, room to run

OBJECT: Catch the ball.

Put the ball in the toe of the sock and tie a knot right above the ball. Choose one person to be the first comet launcher, then have her swing the sock around and around and let it go. Other players try to catch the comet ball by grabbing for the tail as it flies by. Whoever catches it becomes the comet launcher. If no one catches the comet ball, the first comet launcher gets to throw again.

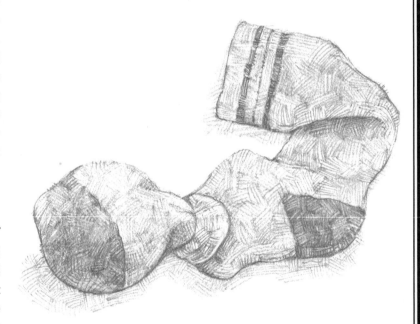

Tips

• It's easier to grab hold of the ball when it's coming back down toward the ground, rather than when it's at the peak of its arc. Envision where the arc will end and move into position there.

Variations

• Turn this into a game of catch.

• Have a competition to see who can throw the comet ball the farthest.

• Have two players throw the comet ball back and forth, with a third player in the middle trying to catch it.

Crack Up

WHO: 5 or more players

WHAT YOU NEED: a bouncing ball such as a kickball

OBJECT: Be the last person out.

. . . .

One person is chosen to be It. It throws the ball at one of the other players, who can either dodge the ball or catch it. If a player gets hit by the ball, he loses a point. If he catches the ball, It loses a point. If the targeted person doesn't catch the ball, any other player can then catch the ball and he becomes It. When a player has accumulated five negative points, he's out of the game. Play continues until there is only one player left; that player is the winner.

Dodgeball

WHO: 6–20 players, divided into two teams

WHAT YOU NEED: 6 large, soft bouncing balls such as a beach ball (an official dodgeball is an 8.25-inch rubber-coated foam ball); a large space (ideally 60 x 30 feet) such as a basketball or tennis court, gymnasium, lawn, or beach area, marked with a center line, end lines, and an attack line on either side, three feet from the center line; tape or chalk to mark the lines; a whistle or someone to shout "Go!"

OBJECT: Eliminate all opposing players by hitting them with the balls.

. . . .

Place the balls evenly along the length of the center line, then have the teams line up along their end lines. At the signal, teams rush to grab the three balls on their right side of the center line and return with the balls to their attack lines. For three minutes, players then try to hit their opponents with the balls. If a player catches a ball in his hands, it does not count as a hit. When a player is hit, he must leave the court. The team that eliminates all opposing players or the team with the fewest eliminated players at the end of the three minutes wins the game.

Additional Rules

1. You may not hold any one ball for longer than ten seconds.

2. A team cannot hold all six balls for longer than five seconds.

3. Aim for shoulders or lower. In some games, players who hit an opponent in the head are immediately out.

Variations

• Bombardment: When a player is hit by a ball, she goes to the opponents' team and tries to catch balls thrown by teammates. If she catches a ball before it touches the ground, she goes back to her own team.

• Indoor Dodgeball: All players form a circle and someone is chosen to be It. That person tosses a soft ball, such as a sponge ball or beach ball, to someone in the circle. If that player catches the ball, he tosses it to someone else. If he drops it, he has to sit down. Last person standing is the winner.

• Killer: When you get hit or the ball you threw is caught, you have to go to your opponents' side. If you're not in place within ten seconds or if you get hit again, you're out of the game.

• One team makes a circle, and the other team stands inside that circle. Players in the circle throw balls at the players in the middle, trying to hit them. Anyone who gets hit with the ball joins the players in the outer circle, and play continues until only one person is left inside the circle.

Fun Facts: Dodgeball is a favorite game of children in Japan.

Five Hundred
(also called Five Dollars)

WHO: 3 or more players

WHAT YOU NEED: any kind of ball, but preferably one that bounces

OBJECT: Be the first to get 500 points.

One person is a thrower, and everyone else is a catcher. A ball can be caught "dead" (after touching the ground) or "alive" (in the air). The thrower throws the ball and calls out how many points it's worth and whether it should be caught dead, alive, or either. For example, the thrower may throw the ball and say, "Twenty-five points, dead!" and the person who catches the ball after it has touched the ground gets 25 points. If they fumble and drop the ball, they lose the points. First person to get 500 points wins the game and becomes the new thrower.

Variations

• Let 100 be the goal so more people get to throw.

• Use a Ping-Pong ball and have the thrower bounce it off the floor instead of throwing it. Whoever catches the Ping-Pong ball after that first bounce gets whatever number of points the thrower says, but if it bounces more than once, whoever catches it gets only half that many points.

• If you have a really big space to play in, have the thrower use a tennis racket to hit a tennis ball into the air.

• Choose a batter; everyone else is a fielder. The batter throws the ball in the air and bats it, and the fielders try to catch it. The first fielder to get 500 points gets to be the next batter, and everybody else goes back to zero points. Points are awarded as follows:

> • Ball is caught before it hits the ground: 100 points
>
> • Ball is caught after one bounce: 75 points
>
> • Ball is caught after two bounces: 50 points
>
> • Catch a grounder or a ball that bounces multiple times: 25 points
>
> • Fumble a fly: Lose 100 points
>
> • Fumble a ball that bounced once: Lose 75 points
>
> • Fumble a ball that bounced twice: Lose 50 points
>
> • Fumble a grounder: Lose 25 points

Four Square
(also called Boxball, Champ, and Squareball)

WHO: 4 or more players

WHAT YOU NEED: a bouncing ball such as a volleyball, soccer ball, or basketball

OBJECT: Get in Square 1.

. . . .

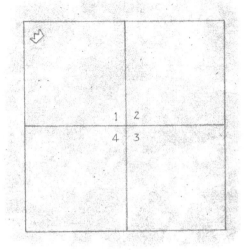

Create a square that is at least 8 x 8 feet and divide it into four equal, smaller squares. (You can use string, chalk, or masking tape to mark the boundaries.) The upper left square is designated as Square 1, with the other squares designated as 2, 3, and 4 as you move clockwise. One person claims each square. The player in Square 1 serves the ball by bouncing it inside her square and then hitting it with her open palms into any one of the other three squares. The player in the square in which the ball lands must then send the ball into a different square, either before it bounces or after only one bounce. Play continues until someone fails to pass the ball or lets it bounce more than once in their square. When a player is out, she goes to either Square 4 or the end of the waiting line if there are more players. The remaining three players advance their squares so that the player in Square 4 moves to Square 3 and so on. A new player always goes to Square 4, and the player in Square 1 always begins the game.

Additional Rules
. . . .

1. Hitting with a fist is not allowed.

2. If the ball bounces on the outside line or outside the four squares, the player who hit it there is out.

3. If the ball bounces on the line between two squares, the other players and those waiting in line can help decide whose square it was in.

4. If a defender catches the ball, gets hit by the ball, lets the ball bounce more than once before she hits it, or lets the ball bounce in her square after she has hit it, she is out.

5. If a ball doesn't bounce in the square it was served to and the defender doesn't return it, the last person to touch the ball is out.

Variations

- The player in Square 1, sometimes called the King or Ace, can modify the rules at the beginning of each new round of play. There are many rule modifications and terms unique to specific geographical areas that can be incorporated into this game.

- Decide on a category: animals, cities, colors, movies, etc. The player in Square 1 calls out an example of the category as she bounces the ball into one of the other three squares. The player in that square then calls out another example as she bounces the ball into a different square. If someone can't think of an example for the category or repeats a word that has already been used, he is out and a new player gets to have that square.

- If you have eight or more players, put two players in each square. Whenever one player hits the ball to another square, she jumps out of the square and her partner jumps in to replace her. The two players switch places every time the ball is hit toward their square.

Fun Facts: Four Square is such a popular game that there are world championships held every February in Bridgton, Maine. For more information, visit www.squarefour.org.

Horse

WHO: 2 or more players

WHAT YOU NEED: a basketball, a basketball hoop

OBJECT: Be the last person to acquire the letters that spell *HORSE*.

Players line up. Player 1 shoots from any position he chooses. If he misses, he gets an *H* and goes to the end of the line, and Player 2 gets to shoot from any position he chooses. If Player 1 makes the basket, he goes to the end of the line and Player 2 must attempt a shot from the same position. If Player 2 makes the basket, then Player 3 (or Player 1, if there are only two players) must attempt a shot from the same position. If Player 2 misses, he gets an *H* and goes to the end of the line. Once a person acquires all the letters required to spell *HORSE*, he is out of the game.

Keep-Away

(also called Monkey in the Middle, Pickle in the Middle, Piggy in the Middle, and Lummelen)

WHO: 3 or more players

WHAT YOU NEED: a bouncing ball such as a kickball or playground ball, room to move around

OBJECT: Try to catch the ball.

Choose one person to be It. The other players form a big circle around her. Players throw the ball back and forth, trying to keep It from touching or catching the ball. If she catches the ball, or if the ball touches her, whoever last threw the ball becomes It. The game ends whenever people are tired of playing.

Variations

- The ball must bounce once before being caught.

- Players must throw the ball within a certain length of time (five seconds, for example). If they don't, they become It.

- People forming the circle must stand still and not move around.

- Instead of having an It standing inside a circle, divide players into teams, give the ball to one team, and have them move around, trying to pass the ball from one teammate to another without the other team getting the ball. If a rival player gets the ball, his team then takes control of it.

- In Africa, this variation of the game is called Mbube, Mbube (the Zulu word for *lion*): Choose one player to be a lion and one player to be an impala. Blindfold both of them and spin them around. Other players form a circle around the lion and the impala and begin calling out "Mbube, mbube!" (pronounced *Mboo-bay*). Whenever the impala gets close to the lion, players' voices get faster and louder, but if the impala moves away, the chants get slower and softer. If the lion catches the impala within one minute, a new impala is selected; if not, a new lion is selected.

Fun Facts: Some version of Keep-Away is played in almost every country of the world, and it's been around since at least the seventeenth century.

Kickball

WHO: 8 or more players

WHAT YOU NEED: a large rubber ball such as a playground ball or soccer ball, something to mark the bases, room to run

OBJECT: Score more points than your opponent.

Kickball is played like softball or baseball, with players kicking the ball instead of hitting it, then running around bases and coming home to score a point.

Set up your bases, divide into teams, and choose positions. The pitcher rolls the ball toward home plate. A bad roll is a ball, a missed roll is a strike, three strikes and the kicker is out, four balls and the kicker gets to walk to first base. The kicker kicks the ball and tries to run to each base before being tagged by an opponent. If he's tagged, he's out. If he gets to the base without being tagged, he's safe. Play is done in innings, with each team allowed three outs. The team with the highest score at the end of an agreed-upon number of innings is the winner.

Variations

- Ignore the three outs rule and let everyone on the team have a chance to kick before the next team comes up to kick.

- Don't call balls or strikes; let every kicker have three chances to kick.

Line Baseball

(also called Line Ball and Over the Line)

WHO: 4 or more players

WHAT YOU NEED: a softball (or small rubber ball), 2 bats

OBJECT: Try to get your ball past the opposing team's lineup.

Decide which team will start. Each team forms a line, thirty feet apart. The first player tosses the ball up and bats it, trying to get it through the other team's lineup. The opposing team tries to field the ball and bat it back through the other team's lineup. Each member of each team gets a chance to bat. One point is scored for each ball that crosses the other team's goal line.

Variations

• Have a pitcher pitch to a batter from the same team instead of having the batter toss the ball up in the air.

• If you don't have bats, you can just throw the ball back and forth.

One Old Cat
(also called Cat Ball, Old Cat, and One-Eyed Cat)

WHO: 4 or more players

WHAT YOU NEED: a bat, a ball, something to mark home plate and one base

OBJECT: Hit the ball and run to the base without getting tagged.

This is like baseball, only the game goes a lot faster since there's only one base involved.

Decide who will be the pitcher, catcher, batter, and fielders. The pitcher throws the ball; the batter hits it and tries to run from home plate to the base and back without getting out. If she does so, she gets a point. If she's out, the next person gets to bat. The batter is out if she gets three strikes, if a fielder throws the ball and hits her, if a fielder tags her or the base with the ball, if a fielder catches her ball on the fly, or if the catcher catches the ball and tags home plate before she gets there. Players take turns rotating from one position to the next. The player who has the most points at the end of the game is the winner.

Fun Facts: One Old Cat has been around since at least the 1800s, and is probably one of the games on which baseball was founded.

Rounders

WHO: 2 teams of equal number (3 people per team minimum)

WHAT YOU NEED: a ball; a bat; a large area such as a field, baseball diamond, or a beach; something to designate 4 bases

OBJECT: Hit the ball and get back home to score a "rounder."

A lot like baseball, this game is for two teams and involves hitting a ball and making your way around three "sanctuaries" (bases) and back to the "castle" (home plate).

One team takes the field and the other team lines up to bat. There are no basemen, only a pitcher and a catcher and fielders, who can stand anywhere *except* on a sanctuary. The pitcher throws an underhand pitch, and the batter swings. Whether he hits the ball or not, he runs to the first sanctuary. A caught fly ball puts him out; any other ball gets thrown to the pitcher, who then throws it on the ground and shouts "Down!" If the player is not on a sanctuary when the pitcher throws the ball down, the runner is out. Every runner that makes it back to the castle scores a point, or a "rounder." Teams trade places whenever one team acquires three outs. The team with the highest score after a predetermined number of innings is the winner.

Additional Rules

1. Only nine people per team should be on the field at one time.

2. There can be more than one runner on a sanctuary at the same time, and runners do not have to move on to the next sanctuary at any particular time.

3. Batting order will constantly change, depending on who is home and who is trying to make a round.

4. If all the players are on a sanctuary, the last player to bat goes back to the castle to bat again. He continues to bat until another player makes it in.

Variations

• Play with a soft rubber ball and no bat, and let batters use their hands to hit the ball.

Fun Facts: Rounders originated in England and has been played there since the 1700s. It's a favorite game of both children and adults in England and Ireland.

Sock Ball

WHO: 1 or more players

WHAT YOU NEED: a small rubber ball, a sock, a wall to stand against

OBJECT: Complete a verse while swinging the ball around.

. . . .

The first player puts the ball inside the sock and stands with her back against the wall. Holding the ankle of the sock (with the ball in the toe) at waist height, she swings the ball back and forth on either side of her body while reciting this verse:

> *A*, my name is Abby (Alice, Annette, Agatha, any name starting with *A*).
> My father's name is Andy (Arnie, Abraham, etc.).
> We come from Alaska (Albertville, Albuquerque, etc.).
> We sell apricots (aardvarks, aspirin, etc.).

If the player completes the rhyme without fumbling for a name or without hitting herself with the ball or getting tangled up in the sock, she continues with the next letter of the alphabet. ("*B*, my name is Bridget. My father's name is Buckwheat. We come from Belize. We sell bagels.") That player makes her way through a verse for each letter until she can't think of a word or there's a mishap with the sock ball. When that happens, it's the next player's turn, or if there's only one player, she starts over at *A*.

Variations

. . . .

- Alternate between swinging the ball at your waist and under your legs. For example, on the first and third lines of the verse, swing the ball at waist level so it hits the wall on either side of your body. On the second line of the rhyme, instead of swinging the sock ball back and forth at your waist, lift your right leg and swing the ball under and over it so it hits the wall on either side.

On the third verse, swing at your waist again, then on the fourth verse, lift your left leg and swing the ball on either side of it.

• Try bouncing the sock ball between your legs, under each arm, or over your head.

Spud
(also called Baby in the Air)

WHO: 3 or more players

WHAT YOU NEED: a playground ball or beach ball, room to run

OBJECT: Be the last player left in the game.

Define the boundaries of the play area so players will know how far they can run. Number off the players; players must remember their number for the rest of the game. Choose a player to be It and have everyone else form a circle around him. It throws the ball high into the air as he calls out a number. Everyone except the player with that number runs as far away from the ball as possible. The player whose number was called runs to catch the ball. As soon as he catches it, he yells "Spud!" and all other players must immediately freeze in place. The player with the ball then takes three giant steps toward the player closest to him and throws the ball in an effort to hit him. If that player gets hit by the ball, he is penalized by earning the letter *S* and he becomes It. (Trying to dodge the ball is not allowed; a player who does not remain frozen will be penalized by earning a letter.) If the ball misses him, the player who threw the ball gets an *S* and becomes It. Play continues as before, with all players forming a circle around the new It. A player who acquires all four letters of the word *SPUD* is out of the game. The game ends when only one player is left.

Variations

• It counts to ten while the other players run away, and everyone freezes when he says "ten." He takes three giant steps toward the closest player, then tries to hit him with the ball. If that player gets hit, he gets an *S* and becomes It. If It misses, he gets an *S* and remains It for another turn.

• Instead of assigning numbers, just use everyone's name.

• For Baby in the Air, spell out *BABY* instead of *SPUD*.

Stickball

(also called Fungo and Wall Ball)

WHO: 2 or more players

WHAT YOU NEED: any stick (broom handle, tree branch, etc.) about the length of a baseball bat and about an inch in diameter, a small rubber ball, something to mark the bases, room to run

OBJECT: Get the most points.

Essentially, stickball is a variation of baseball, and the same general rules apply. One person is chosen to be the batter, a pitcher is an optional position, and everyone else fields. Depending on which variation you play, the batter either throws the ball up in the air to hit it or a pitcher pitches it to him, and the fielders try to catch it. Typically, there are no bases (see Variations). You can play a predetermined number of innings, or simply end the game when people get tired of playing.

Additional Rules

1. One, two, or three strikes and you're out; decide beforehand.

2. Batters cannot strike out looking; they only swing at balls they like.

3. Fouls and tips count as strikes.

4. There are no called balls.

5. If you hit the ball way out of the playing area, you have to go get it!

6. Lobbing the ball through a window or over a roof is either an automatic out or automatic home run; decide beforehand.

Variations

- With lots of people, you can play on teams. With just a few, you can track your points individually.

- If there's no room to run bases, you can determine points by the distance of a hit. For example, if the ball goes past the rosebush, it's one point; past the big rock, two points; past the pecan tree, three points; past the road, four points.

- Fungo is when the batter throws the ball up in the air himself (or bounces it once or twice) and then hits it.

- Fast-pitch stickball (also called Wall Ball) requires a wall of some sort behind the batter so a strike zone can be designated with tape or chalk. The pitcher throws an overhand ball directly at the batter, and the number of bases earned is determined by how far the ball is hit, not by actually running bases.

- In slow-pitch stickball, you don't count balls or strikes; every batter simply gets two swings, period. The pitcher throws the ball so that it bounces once, then the batter tries to hit it.

Fun Facts: Stickball originated as a city game played in neighborhood streets and dates back to the 1700s. The stick was usually a mop or broom handle—often with tape wrapped around one end for a better grip—and bases were often garbage cans, manhole covers, and parked wagons or, later, cars. Native Americans played stickball as well, often using the game as a way to settle disputes.

Stoopball
(also called Curb Ball)

WHO: 1 or more players

WHAT YOU NEED: a small rubber ball, some steps or a curb

OBJECT: Catch the ball and rack up points.

Stand five to ten feet from the steps (or curb, if no steps are available), throw the ball, and try to catch it as it bounces off the steps. If you're playing with partners and fail to catch the ball, your turn is over.

Bounce the ball off the step and catch it after one bounce—5 points

Bounce the ball off the step and catch it on the rebound—10 points

Bounce the ball off the edge of the step and catch it on the rebound—100 points

The goal can be whatever you agree on; 100, 500, and 1000 points are common goals. If you reach the goal, keep playing until you miss a ball; you are then officially out of the game and your partners have a chance to get in their "last licks" to see if they can get more points before missing a ball and being out of the game as well.

Variations

• Set a time limit (such as a minute) and see who can get the most points in that period of time.

• Lose a point for every ball you miss.

• If your ball bounces more than once, lose all your points.

Fun Facts: Stoopball has always been a favorite game of city kids who don't have playgrounds handy. Instead, they use the sidewalks, streets, or front stoops (steps) of their apartments and houses to create a play area. The favorite ball to use, originally, was either a Spalding Hi-Bounce Ball (nicknamed the Spaldeen) or a Pensie Pinkie (called the Pinky). Small, pink, lightweight, and very bouncy, one brand or the other could be found in almost every home with children from the late 1940s until production stopped in 1979. Spalding began manufacturing the balls again—in multiple colors—in 1999.

Twenty-One
(also called Straight Up)

WHO: 2 players

WHAT YOU NEED: a basketball, a basketball hoop, tape or chalk to mark a free throw line 10–15 feet in front of the hoop

OBJECT: Get the ball through the hoop.

One player stands under the hoop, and the other player (the shooter) stands right behind the free throw line. The shooter throws the ball and tries to get it in the basket. If she does, she scores 2 points. If she misses, the player under the basket tries to retrieve the ball, dribble it back to the basket, and shoot it in while the other player tries to block him. If he's successful, he scores 1 point and then gets a turn at the free throw line. If he misses, the original shooter gets another turn. The first player to exactly 21 points wins. If a player goes over 21 points, she goes back to zero points.

Fun Facts: The game of basketball was invented by James Naismith in 1891. A Canadian who grew up on a peach farm, he nailed peach baskets to the end walls of a gym and, voilà, the first basketball hoops were born!

Alphabet Traveler

WHO: 2 or more players

WHAT YOU NEED: your thinking cap

OBJECT: Be the last person out.

. . . .

Decide who will start, then have each player take a turn at saying "I'm going to [someplace that starts with an *A*] to [do some activity that starts with an *A*] [an adjective that starts with an *A*][a noun that starts with an *A*]." For example, "I'm going to Alabama to act in an airy amphitheater." (You can add words like "in an" or "to the" to make your sentence work!) As soon as everyone has had a turn, devote the next round to the next letter in the alphabet. For example, "I'm going to Belgium to box belching buffalo," then "I'm going to church to capture crawly caterpillars." Try to keep playing until you get all the way to Z.

Additional Rules

. . . .

1. The letter *X* can be skipped

2. Players who cannot come up with a sentence within sixty seconds are out of the game.

Association

WHO: 2 or more players

WHAT YOU NEED: your thinking cap

OBJECT: Think of a word related to the one you just heard.

. . . .

One player calls out a word, and the next player immediately calls out a word that is somehow associated with the first word. Play continues until everyone is tired of the game. For example: shoulder, arm, leg, knee, scrape, ice, winter, summer, sun, beach, whale, etc. Words must have some direct connection to the previous word, and anyone who fails to come up with a word is out of the game.

Bird, Beast, Fish

WHO: 2 or more players

WHAT YOU NEED: a piece of paper, a pen or pencil for each player

OBJECT: Guess the word.

One player thinks of an animal (bird, beast, or fish) and on his piece of paper draws a line for each letter of the word. He fills in two letters, then shows the paper to the other players, who take turns trying to guess the correct animal. Whoever guesses gets to think of the next bird, beast, or fish.

Tips

• You can set a time limit (one minute per person, for example) or limit the number of guesses (perhaps three times around) to keep the game moving. If no one has guessed by then, the person can announce what the animal was and choose a new one, or the turn can move on to the next player.

Botticelli

WHO: 3 or more players

WHAT YOU NEED: your thinking cap

OBJECT: Guess the mysterious famous person.

Decide who will start. That person thinks of a famous person or character (living or dead, real or fictional) and announces the initial of that person's last name. Players begin guessing by asking yes-or-no questions that describe the famous person. For example, let's say the chooser said, "My person's name begins with *B*" and he has chosen Batman. The first guesser might be thinking it's Barney the Dinosaur, and would ask, "Is he purple?" The chooser would answer, "No, I'm not Barney," and the next player would ask a question. If the chooser can't think of a specific famous person to rule out, though, and can only answer yes or no to a guesser's question, then the person who asked that question gets to ask *another* question before his turn ends. This happens any time the chooser has to resort to a yes or no answer.

Tips

- When it's your turn to choose a famous person, try to select someone you know a lot about.

- If you're trying to guess, make your questions very general so the chooser will have a hard time thinking of something other than a yes or no answer.

- To simplify the game, give the initials of the famous person's first *and* last name.

Fun Facts: This game is named after the famous Italian painter Sandro Botticelli, who is *so* famous that, theoretically, *everyone* knows who he was. Anyone you think of should be at least as well-known as Botticelli.

Categories

WHO: 4 or more players

WHAT YOU NEED: your thinking cap

OBJECT: Be the last person left in the game.

Choose someone to start. That person slaps his hands on his knees twice while saying "Categories," then claps twice while saying "such as," then snaps the fingers of one hand then the other while naming some category, such as movies, books, animals, foods, etc. The next person does a slap slap, then a clap clap, then names something in that category as they snap snap. For example:

> "Categories . . . such as . . . salad dressings."
> "Ranch."
> "Thousand Island."
> "Honey mustard."

When it gets back to the person who started the category, the person on his left names a new category. If you can't think of something in the category, if you repeat something that's already been said, or if you fail to offer up a suggestion within one minute, you're out of the game. Continue playing until only one person remains.

Variations

• You can leave off all the slapping and clapping and snapping and just let people take turns naming something in a category.

Charades

WHO: 5 or more players

WHAT YOU NEED: paper cut into strips, a pen or pencil, a bowl or basket, a timer

OBJECT: Act out a phrase or word as other players try to guess what it is.

Have everyone write down the names of famous people, book/movie/song/TV show titles, or familiar expressions on strips of paper, with their name written underneath. Put all suggestions in a bowl or basket. Then have the first player choose one without looking at it and announce the name of the person who wrote down that suggestion; the person who suggested the charade is not allowed to play in that round. Using only the approved gestures (see next page) and without talking, the first player acts out clues to help other players guess the charade within three minutes.

Additional Rules

1. You can point and use props, body movement, or facial expressions, but absolutely no talking is allowed by the person doing the charade. First she acts out the category, then moves on to act out either the entire phrase or individual words. Standard pantomime gestures are listed below.

2. As people call out guesses, the actor must respond immediately, either shaking his head for an incorrect guess or touching the tip of his nose (or nodding) for a correct one.

3. Whoever guesses correctly gets to act out the next charade. If no one guesses the charade within three minutes, the actor announces what the word or phrase was and the person to his right chooses a charade.

Categories

- Book: Hold your hands open like a book.

- Movie: Make fists with both hands. Place one in front of you and wind the other around it on one side, like an old-fashioned movie camera.

- Person: Put your hand inside your shirt, mimicking the pose made famous by Napoléon Bonaparte.

- Place: Make circles with your hands and put them in front of your eyes like binoculars.

- Slogan or Expression: Hold up two fingers from each hand and pretend to make quotation marks in the air.

- Song: Mimic singing, with your mouth open and your hands outstretched.

- TV Show: Use your fingers to draw a square in the air.

Hints

- Entire phrase: Cross your arms over your chest, or wave your arms around in a huge circle.

- Future tense of a word: Hold your hand above your eyes, like you're trying to look at something far away, and lean forward.

- Little word (such as *a*, *it*, *on*, *the*, etc.): Hold your thumb and index finger close together.

- Longer version of a word: Put the fingers of each hand together and make a stretching motion, like pulling taffy.

- Number of words in a phrase: Hold up a finger for however many words there are.

- Past tense of a word: Hold your hand above your eyes, like you're trying to look at something far away, and look over your shoulder or wave your hand behind your back.

- Shorter version of a word: Put your palms very close together.

- Syllable: On one forearm, lay down a finger for every syllable of a word. (For *Bambi*, you'd lay down two fingers.) Then, to act out a clue for the second syllable—the *bi* part, in the case of *Bambi*—lay down two fingers on your forearm again.

- Word sounds like: Cup your hand around your ear, then act out the word *your* word sounds like.

- You're getting close: Make a "come on" motion with one or both hands.

Variations

- If you have lots of people, you can divide into teams, and then the entire team can brainstorm and guess when their representative is doing the charade. You can also have two teams doing a specific number of charades simultaneously; the team to finish their charades first, or to acquire the greatest number of correct answers, wins.

- You can limit the categories to just one, such as movie titles, to make things simpler.

Fun Facts: Charades is known as a parlor game (a game to be played indoors), and has been around since the sixteenth century. The game originated in France.

Dumb Crambo

(also called ABC of Aristotle, Capping the Rhyme, and Crambo)

WHO: 4 or more players

WHAT YOU NEED: pencil and paper to keep score

OBJECT: Try to guess a word as it's acted out—with no talking allowed!

Divide players into two groups. Team one will choose a mystery word, and team two will try to guess it. Team two is sent to another room or a distant spot while team one huddles to choose a word. You'll want to choose a word that has plenty of words that rhyme with it. (If you pick *carry*, for example, that rhymes with *berry, tarry, hairy, fairy, cherry, dairy, marry, nary, prairie*, etc.)

When team one is ready, they call team two back to join them. Then they announce one word that rhymes with their chosen word. Team two huddles for a moment to think of three possible words that could be the mystery word, then they act out those words, one by one. For example, they might act out the word *marry* by mimicking familiar wedding ceremony rituals, such as putting rings on fingers or kissing the bride. Members of team one will hiss and shake their heads because their chosen word is not *marry*. Then team two might act out the word *hairy* by acting like apes, pretending to shave their legs or chins, or flinging their hair about. Team one would again hiss and shake their heads. On their last chance, let's say team two chooses the word *carry* to act out. They might mimic carrying pails of water, carrying one another on their backs, or carrying objects across the room. This time, team one will cheer and applaud because team two guessed correctly. If a team correctly guesses the word, they get 1 point. If they do not, the other team gets a point. The first team to get 10 points wins.

Additional Rules

1. No talking is allowed during pantomimes.

2. A team gets to guess and act out only three words.

3. Teams switch places after each round of guessing.

Variations

• Instead of teams silently pantomiming to guess the words, one person thinks of a word and says, "I know a word that rhymes with *jack*" (for example, or any other word). Other players then try to guess the word by asking questions, and the thinker must respond with a sentence that ends with a rhyming word. For example, if the word is *black*, someone might guess, "Is it sharp?" and the thinker would respond, "It's not a tack." Someone else might guess, "Does it hurt?" and the thinker would say, "It's not a smack." Play continues until someone guesses the word or until players run out of guesses. The player who guesses correctly gets to think of the next word.

Fun Facts: This is a parlor game that dates back to the fourteenth century and was especially popular during the Victorian age. It's called Dumb Crambo because the word *dumb* means mute, or unable to speak.

Fortunately/Unfortunately

WHO: 2 or more players

WHAT YOU NEED: your thinking cap

OBJECT: Keep the game going.

The person who begins is an optimist, and the next person is a pessimist. Alternate as you give sentences. The optimist makes a statement such as "Fortunately, the sun is shining today." The pessimist continues the story, but introduces a negative element, such as, "Unfortunately, it's supposed to rain tonight." Then the next person gives a positive sentence: "Fortunately, we have umbrellas for everyone." And the next person gives a negative sentence: "Unfortunately, the umbrellas are locked in the closet, and we've lost the key." The game continues until you get tired of it.

Geography

WHO: 2 or more players

WHAT YOU NEED: your thinking cap

OBJECT: Be the last player left in the game.

The first player names a geographical thing—a city, state, country, body of water, island, mountain, etc. The next player names a geographical thing that begins with the last letter of the word used by the first player. For example, if player one says "Mount Rushmore," the next player could say "Everglades," and player three could say "Straits of Gibraltar," and player four could say "Rome." If a player repeats a word that's already been used or if he cannot think of a word, he is out of the game. The last person remaining in the game is the winner.

Variations

- You can play this game with other categories, such as TV shows, movie stars, books, sports-related things, or food.

Hangman

(also called Gallows)

WHO: 2 or more players

WHAT YOU NEED: pencil and paper for all players

OBJECT: Guess the word before you get hanged.

Decide who will be the first hangman. That player thinks of a word and, on a sheet of paper, draws a simple gallows. Underneath it, she draws a dash for each letter of the word. For example, if the word is *elephant*, the player draws eight dashes. The other players take turns trying to guess the word, one letter at a time. If they guess a correct letter, the hangman writes that letter above all the dashes where that letter would appear. If a player guesses a letter that is not in the word, the hangman writes that letter underneath the dashes, then draws a head on the gallows. Each time someone incorrectly guesses a letter, the hangman draws another body part. (Body parts should be drawn in this order: head, torso, left arm, right arm, left leg, right leg.) Players may guess a word instead of a letter when it is their turn. If the guess is incorrect, the hangman draws a new body part, just as she does when it's an incorrect letter. If someone correctly guesses the word or identifies the last missing letter, that person gets to be the next hangman. If no one guesses the word before the drawing is completed, the hangman announces what it was and gets to think of another word.

Tips

• Guessing all the vowels first can make it easier to identify a word.

• The most common letters are, in order, *E, T, A, O, I, N, S, R, H, L, D.*

Variations

- To provide more guessing opportunities, you may start with a blank sheet of paper and use drawing the gallows as part of the game. You may also choose to add facial features to the body.

- You may try to guess familiar phrases (like "day and night" or "because I said so") instead of single words, or even movie or book titles.

Fun Facts: Hangman has been played since at least the 1800s. The popular TV game show *Wheel of Fortune* is based on this game.

Hink Pink

WHO: 2 or more players

WHAT YOU NEED: your thinking cap

OBJECT: Keep making rhymes as long as you can.

Hink Pinks are one-syllable rhyming word riddles. One player or team offers a two-word description of something, and the other player or team has to respond with a Hink Pink. For example, the first player might say "amphibian hangout," and the other player would reply with "frog bog."

Variations

- Make this game even more challenging by coming up with Hinky Pinkies: two-syllable word riddles ("smelly primate" = "funky monkey").

- Make it crazy-hard by playing Hinkety Pinketies: three-syllable word riddles ("outrageous story" = "terrible parable").

I Spy

WHO: 3 or more players

WHAT YOU NEED: your eyes

OBJECT: Guess what someone else has spied.

Decide who will start. That person looks around, selects an object that is visible to all players, and says, "I spy, with my little eye, something that is [name the color of the object]." The other players then take turns guessing what the object might be. For example, if the spier spots a yellow pencil on a table, she would say, "I spy, with my little eye, something that is yellow." Someone might guess, "Jerry's shirt?" The spier would say no, then the next person would offer a guess. If no one guesses in the first round, then the spier can offer up another clue before players guess again. For example, "I spy, with my little eye, something that is yellow and straight." (Or yellow and pink, if the pencil has a pink eraser, or yellow and skinny, etc.) The player who correctly guesses the object wins that round and gets to choose the next object.

Tips

• Unless you are trying to make the game especially easy, try to choose an object that is the same color as several other objects. If there's only one red thing in the room, it won't take much effort to figure it out!

Variations

• Instead of colors, choose objects that begin with a specific letter of the alphabet, and work your way from A to Z. For example, "I spy, with my little eye, something that begins with A." (It might be an apple, an air freshener, or almonds.)

Fun Facts: I Spy has been played since at least the early 1900s, and versions of it are played all over the world. It inspired a hugely popular book series in England in the 1950s, in which children tried to find and document specific objects listed in the pages, then sent in their completed book to receive a prize. Another I Spy series, featuring photographic collages and rhymes, was launched in the United States in 1991 and continues to thrive.

Memory Game

WHO: 3 or more players

WHAT YOU NEED: a tray, 10–20 small objects that can fit on the tray (such as jewelry, candy, toys, coins, flowers, etc.), pencil and paper for each player

OBJECT: Remember what you saw on the tray.

. . . .

Have someone who is not playing arrange all the items on the tray while everyone else sits down with their paper and pencil. The person with the tray slowly carries it around the room so that every player has a chance to see, up close, what is on the tray. The tray is then removed from the room, and everyone has two minutes to write down as many items as they can remember. The player who remembers the most items wins. If there is a tie for who remembered the most, the person with the most descriptive details wins; for example, if one person has "clothespin" and the other has "red clothespin," the player who included the color would win.

Variations

. . . .

• Instead of carrying a tray in and out of the room, you can assemble the memory items on a countertop or table, let players spend a minute or two studying them, then cover the items with a towel.

Rigmarole

WHO: 2 or more players

WHAT YOU NEED: your thinking cap

OBJECT: Come up with and remember three-word phrases that all start with the same letter.

Choose a player to start. That person must use the word *one* and two other words that start with *O* in a three-word phrase. For example, "one ordinary olive" or "one oblong opossum." The next player repeats that phrase, then adds a phrase of his own, using the word *two*. For example, "one ordinary olive, two tall turkeys." Players take turns repeating the previous phrases and adding one of their own until you get to ten, after which you start again at one. Any player who leaves out a phrase, repeats it incorrectly, or forgets to add a new one is out of the game. The last player remaining in the game is the winner.

Variations

• Make this game more difficult (and more fun!) by making the number of words in the phrase match the number. For example: "one orangutan," "two ticklish tadpoles," "three thin theatrical thieves," etc.

Telephone
(also called Gossip)

WHO: 5 or more players (the more people, the more fun!)

WHAT YOU NEED: good ears

OBJECT: Try to accurately communicate a message.

Have all players sit in a circle. Have one player think of a short sentence, such as "I rarely see ghosts in the dark." (She can write down the sentence on a piece of paper to make sure she remembers it correctly, but no one else should see what is written.) Now have that player whisper her sentence into the ear of the player on her right. The player on her right then whispers what he heard to the player on *his* right. The sentence is whispered around the circle, one person

at a time. No one is allowed to say the sentence more than once, so players must listen carefully. The last person then says aloud what he thinks he heard, after which the first player will announce her original sentence. The two sentences may be quite different!

The Minister's Cat

(also called the Prime Minister's Cat and the Preacher's Cat)

WHO: 2 or more players

WHAT YOU NEED: your thinking cap

OBJECT: Keep the game going.

Decide who will start. Everyone starts clapping in a steady rhythm, and the first person says, "The minister's cat is an _____ cat," filling in the blank with an adjective that starts with *A*. For example, "The minister's cat is an arrogant cat." One by one, all other players take a turn, adding their own adjective that begins with *A*. When all players have had a turn, the player who started repeats the sentence again, this time using an adjective that begins with *B*. Play continues until all letters of the alphabet have been used. Anyone who can't think of an adjective or repeats one that has already been used is out of the game.

Variations

• To make things faster, each player can choose the next letter of the alphabet instead of using the same one. For example, the first player might say, "The minister's cat is an arrogant cat," player two might say, "The minister's cat is a beautiful cat," player three might say, "The minister's cat is a creepy cat," etc.

• Play without clapping.

Fun Facts: The Minister's Cat was popular during the 1800s, and a wonderful example of it is included in the 1970 musical *Scrooge*, starring Albert Finney and Alec Guinness.

Tic-Tac-Toe

(also called Naughts and Crosses and X's and O's)

WHO: 2 players

WHAT YOU NEED: paper, 2 pencils

OBJECT: Be the first person to get three X's or three O's in a row.

. . . .

On the paper, draw four straight lines—two down and two across—so that you create nine squares. The first player draws an X in any square; the second player draws an O in any square. Players continue alternating turns, trying to complete a row of three of their symbol in any direction (down, across, or diagonally). As soon as a player puts the third X or O in a row, he draws a line through all three letters. The first person to create a row wins that round, and the loser starts the next round.

Tips

. . . .

• If you go first, put your first two marks in corner squares.

• It's harder to win if you go second. Aim for a tie by blocking every row your opponent starts.

Fun Facts: Carved images of the nine-square grid have been found in archeological sites dating back to the first century BC. Tic-Tac-Toe was also the first computer game ever developed, so it's a very significant part of our culture!

Twenty Questions
(also called Animal, Vegetable, or Mineral)

WHO: 3 or more players

WHAT YOU NEED: your thinking cap

OBJECT: Guess the mystery word.

Pick a player to be the answerer. That person should think of a person, place, or thing for other players to guess by asking questions. The first question should be, "Animal, vegetable, or mineral?" and the answerer will say which one of those categories his word falls into (see below). After that question, players may only ask yes-or-no questions. The answerer may answer with "yes," "no," "maybe," "sometimes," "I don't know," or "I can't answer." Players can ask a total of only twenty questions combined. If a player thinks she knows the answer, she may make a guess instead of asking a question. If she is correct, she gets to choose the next word. If she is not, questioning continues. If no one has identified the object after twenty questions, the answerer reveals the answer and gets to go again.

Categories

• An animal is anything that moves, breathes, or did at one time—so that could be a person, a leather purse, a whale, or a hot dog.

• A vegetable is anything that is, or is made from, a plant—think orange juice, a T-shirt, a bamboo rug, or a banana split.

• A mineral is anything that's never been alive, which covers everything from trucks to buildings to staplers to cameras.

Fun Facts: A radio show based on Twenty Questions aired from 1946–1954, and a TV show called *Twenty Questions* aired from 1949–1954. Various versions of those shows also aired in Canada, England, and Norway. The most frequent question was, "Is it bigger than a bread box?"

Who Am I?

WHO: 3 or more players

WHAT YOU NEED: your thinking cap

OBJECT: Guess the identity of a mysterious person.

. . . .

One player, the guesser, is sent out of the room while the other players decide on a well-known person who may be dead, alive, or fictional. The guesser returns, and each player offers up a clue to the mysterious person's identity. For example, if the person is Superman, the first clue might be "Your girlfriend's name starts with an *L*." The next might be "You work at a newspaper." When every player has offered a clue, the guesser gets three chances to name the mystery person. If he gets it right, he gets to choose the next guesser. If he doesn't, the next guesser is determined at random. The players can also continue to offer more clues to the guesser until he gets the answer.

Tips

. . . .

• Make sure the mystery person you choose is familiar to all players in your group.

• Clues should be helpful, but not too revealing, if you want the game to last. For example, "He's faster than a speeding bullet" would immediately identify Superman.

Balloon Rocket

WHO: just you—but you might want a helper for the setup

WHAT YOU NEED: one oblong balloon, tape, a plastic straw, a long piece (10–20 feet) of kite string or fishing line

OBJECT: Create a rocket that can fly through the air.

Thread the string through the straw. Tie one end of the string to some stationary object (a mailbox, tree, chair, etc.), pull it taut, and tie the other end to another stationary object. Blow up the balloon and hold the end closed with the fingers of one hand. With your other hand, securely tape the side of the balloon to the straw. Slide the balloon and straw back in the direction of the opening on the balloon, all the way to one end of the string, and then release it. The balloon should rocket across the line.

Variations

- Skip the straw and the string and create rocket features from paper (a tube for the balloon to fit into, wings taped onto the tube, a nose cone, etc.). Slip the blown-up balloon inside the rocket, secure it with some tape, and let it go.

- If there are two of you, set up two strings and two balloon rockets side by side and let them race.

Can Stilts

WHO: just you

WHAT YOU NEED: 2 empty cans of the same size, open on one end; a length of clothesline or thin rope about three times your height; scissors to cut the rope; a punch can opener

OBJECT: Have fun balancing and being taller!

Use the can opener to punch two holes in the attached lid of each can, one on either side. Thread the end of the rope into one of the holes in a can. Make a knot in the end you threaded through so that when you pull the other end, the knot sits on the inside of the can, holding the rope in place. Stand on the can and hold up the rope, finding a length that is comfortable but allows good control. The rope should come up from one hole in the can, pass through your hands, and go back down into the other side of the can, creating a loop handle. When you're comfortable with the length, cut off the excess rope, pass the rope through the other hole in the can, and make a knot as you did on the first side. Repeat the procedure for the second can. With the open sides down and the closed ends up, put one foot on each can (with the ropes coming through on either side of your foot), wrap your hands around the rope handles, and pull up to maintain pressure and keep the cans snug against your feet as you walk.

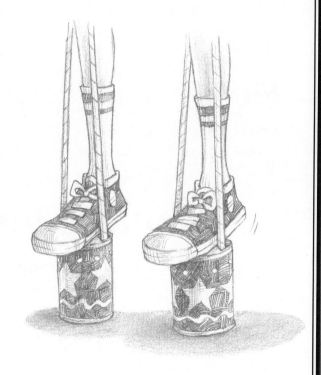

Tips

• Use smaller cans (vegetables, soup) for little feet, and larger ones (coffee, juice) for bigger feet.

• Decorate your cans with colored duct tape, paint, or stickers.

Catch a Coin

WHO: just you

WHAT YOU NEED: any kind of coin

OBJECT: Flip a coin off your elbow and catch it.

Bend your arm so that your elbow is straight out in front of you and your fist is resting, palm up, on your shoulder. Place a coin flat on top of your elbow. Fling your hand down and try to catch the coin before it hits the ground.

Tips

• You may find heavier coins—such as nickels, quarters, fifty-cent pieces, or silver dollars—are easier to work with than lighter ones.

CATCH!

Clothespins in the Bottle

WHO: just you

WHAT YOU NEED: 10 or 20 clothespins, a glass bottle, such as one for juice

OBJECT: See how many clothespins you can get in the bottle

Hold the clothespins in your hands. Stand very straight with your feet together. Place the bottle on the ground right in front of your toes. Holding one clothespin directly over the opening of the bottle, at about waist level, try to drop it straight in. You get a point for every clothespin that goes in the bottle. See how long it takes you to get to a hundred points.

Tips

- You can use a plastic bottle, but a glass one is less likely to tip over.

- To make this game harder, use a bottle with a smaller mouth; to make it easier, use one with a bigger mouth.

- You can store your clothespins in the bottle and just empty them out when you're ready to play.

Cootie Catcher
(also called a Fortune Teller)

WHO: just you

WHAT YOU NEED: a piece of 8 1/2 x 11-inch paper, a pencil or markers, scissors

OBJECT: Entertain people with your ability to predict the future!

Lay the paper in front of you with the short side at the top. Fold the bottom right corner up, so that the edge touches the long, left side of the paper. Press it flat. The folded part will look like a triangle. Cut off the top edge of the paper so that now you really *do* have a triangle.

Open the folded paper. Now you have a square with a diagonal crease from the bottom left to the top right. Fold the bottom left corner of the paper up diagonally, so that the bottom left corner is touching the upper right corner, and press to flatten the fold.

Open the paper again. Now there are *two* creases, like an X in the center of the paper. Fold the bottom left corner so that the tip is touching the center of the X. Press it flat and leave it folded. Now fold the bottom *right* corner in the same way—with the tip touching the center of the X. Press that flat and leave it folded. (Your paper should look like a V at the bottom.) Now do the same thing with the other two corners. When you finish, your paper will look like a smaller square.

Turn the square over so all the corners you just folded are on the bottom side. Fold the new bottom right corner up so the tip touches the center of the square. Press it flat. Do the same thing with each of the other three corners. You should have another smaller square now.

Fold your square in half to create a rectangle and press to flatten all those folded angles. Then unfold it and fold it in half the *other* way, making another rectangle. Open it again to the square with the corners you folded down last.

The folds on the square divide it into eight equal triangles; write a different number (one through eight) in the center of each triangle. Now fold back the four tips. You should see two triangles on each tip, each on the reverse side of the numbers you just wrote. Write a fortune on each triangle—some sort of fun or silly prediction about what might happen to the friends or family members on whom you'll be using your Cootie Catcher. For example: "You are about to have some good luck" or "Beware of an upcoming test!"

Fold the tips back down so the numbers are visible again. Now turn your square over so the numbered side is facedown. The square facing you is divided into four smaller squares by the folds you made. Write the name of a different color on each of these four squares. Now fold the paper in half so that you have two color squares on each side of it. Insert your index fingers and your thumbs into the four flaps under the color names. This should open the paper a little, making it look kind of like a square flower.

To use your Cootie Catcher, have someone choose one of the colors on the outside flaps. Open and close the Cootie Catcher up/down and then sideways, one time for each letter in the color. (If the color is blue, open and close the paper mouth four times, two in each direction; if it's green, five times.) Then have the person choose a number that is visible in the Cootie's mouth, and open and close the Cootie Catcher that many times. The person now selects another number, this time lifting up that number and reading the fortune underneath.

Variations

- Make your Cootie Catcher mysteriously answer questions by writing answers instead of fortunes. On the eight triangles of the tips, write answers such as "yes," "no," "maybe," "you'll have to ask an expert," "I don't think so!" etc.

- You don't have to write colors on the flaps. You can use words you like or that are related to a certain theme. For example, if you wanted to make a superhero Cootie Catcher, you could write *Batman*, *Superman*, *Spider-Man*, and *Iron Man* on the flaps.

Cup Catch

WHO: just you

WHAT YOU NEED: aluminum foil crumpled into a ball, a long piece of string, tape, a cup with a handle

OBJECT: Catch the ball in the cup.

Tie one end of the string to the cup handle. Use the tape to fasten the other end of the string to the foil ball. (You can also tape the string to a flat piece of foil and then crumple the foil into a ball around the string for extra strength.) Hold the cup by the handle and swing the ball up into the air, trying to catch it in the cup.

Fun Facts: Cup Catch was played as a game of skill in ancient India and Greece. It was popular with both children and adults in Europe in the late 1500s, and when the pilgrims came to America, they brought this game with them.

Glider

WHO: just you

WHAT YOU NEED: a piece of 9 x 12-inch construction paper, 2 paper clips, a plastic straw, a pair of scissors

OBJECT: Create a glider that will sail through the air.

Slide a paper clip into either end of the straw, with the larger part of the clip on the inside. Try to position the paper clips so that they are in the same place on either end. Cut two strips down the long side of the paper, one 1 1/2 inches wide, the other 3/4 inch wide. Fold the thinner strip in half lengthwise, then make a circle by bringing the two ends of the paper together. Fasten the two ends into the paper clip on one end of the straw. Make a circle with the other strip as well (but don't fold this one in half), and fasten the ends together in the paper clip at the other end of the straw. Readjust the clips so they are perfectly aligned. You should have a paper circle hanging from each end of the straw, one narrow and one

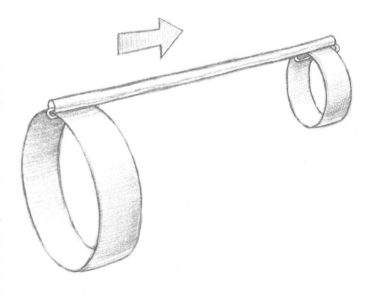

wide. Hold your glider by the middle of the straw with the narrow circle in the front. Extend your arm back and launch it into the air. It should glide through the sky just like a real glider.

Tips

• If it doesn't glide smoothly, make the larger circle smaller by readjusting the diameter with the paper clip. Keep adjusting until it soars like you want it to.

Hand Shadows

WHO: just you

WHAT YOU NEED: your hands, a lamp or flashlight, a light-colored wall, two skinny strips of paper about 4 inches long

OBJECT: Create a whole menagerie to keep you company!

Making hand shadows is a great way to entertain yourself. Just shine a lamp on a wall and move your hands between them to make shadows. Here are some basic shadows you can try. You can probably come up with more of your own; just keep moving your hands around and see what you come up with.

Bird in Flight

Hold both hands in front of you, crossed at the wrist, palms facing you. Press your thumbs together, close your fingers, and extend the palm and fingers of each hand. Make your bird fly by waving your hands gently back and forth.

Crab

Hold your hands up and cross your arms at the wrists. Tuck your thumbs down toward your palms, spread your fingers wide, then curl them slightly.

Crocodile

Put your hands together lengthwise, with your palms and wrists touching. Curl your index finger over the middle finger on the top hand, creating an eye bump. Now curl your ring finger and pinky on that same hand slightly under, creating teeth. Separate your hands just a bit and curl up the thumb, ring finger, and pinky of the bottom hand to make the bottom teeth. You can make your crocodile snap by flexing your hands at the wrist!

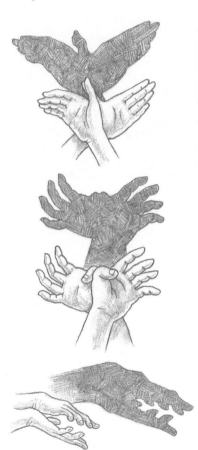

Dog

Hold both your hands in the air with palms together, thumbs sticking up, and fingers facing straight out in front of you. Twist one hand down slightly and, leaving the thumb sticking up, curl your four fingers into your palm to make a slight fist. Curl back your index finger on the other hand, then separate your pinky from the other fingers to create your dog's bottom jaw.

Elephant

Hold one hand in the air and bend it down from the wrist. With your middle finger, ring finger, and thumb hanging down, stick up your index finger and your pinky. Now lay your other hand on top, curving your palm and all five fingers to fit right on top. Bend your fingers slightly at the knuckles, just enough to let through a tiny peep of light for the elephant's eye. You can make the elephant eat by moving the two fingers that are hanging down; have them forage around for a second or two, then curl them up toward your palm and in front of the thumb that's hanging down.

Kangaroo

Hold one hand in the air and bend it straight up from the wrist. Put your thumb slightly forward, hold your index finger straight up, and curve your other three fingers slightly, with your pinky slightly separated from your ring finger. Now place the palm of your other hand against the side of the first hand's wrist, with the thumb sticking up to make the kangaroo's tail and all your fingers curved back into the palm. Leaving the other three fingers curled, extend your pinky to become the kangaroo's feet.

Rabbit

Hold one hand in the air with the palm facing you and the thumb held snugly next to your hand. Curl your index finger back toward your palm, leaving a little hole for light to get through for the rabbit's eye. Hold the other three fingers straight up, with the middle finger separated slightly from the other two. Now place your other hand next to your extended hand, slightly past the wrist, with the palm facing away from you. Curl your ring finger and pinky back into your palm, but keep your thumb, index, and middle finger extended forward and slightly curved to make the bunny's hands and feet.

Rooster

Hold your hands clasped together in front of you, the fingers interlocked. (You might have to straighten your knuckles a bit to make the rooster's comb more obvious.) Extend your thumbs so they're pointing straight back at your face, then rest one thumb on top of the other one to create the rooster's beak.

Snail

Hold out one hand in front of you, with the palm facing away from your face, then bend all your fingers upward. With your other hand, make a fist, then rest the fist on top of the wrist of your raised hand.

Snake

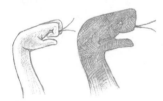

Hold your hand in the air, bent forward at the wrist, with the knuckles straight and the fingers curled into your palm. Move your thumb down under your fingers and hold it there. With your other hand, insert two skinny strips of paper on either side of your middle finger and squeeze your fingers tight to hold them in place.

Tips

• If your walls are painted a dark color, tape a bedsheet or a piece of white paper to the wall to make the shadows show up better.

• You can make a different kind of shadow puppet by drawing the outline of an object (an animal, a truck, a spaceship, a snowman, etc.) on pieces of cardboard (the lid or bottom of a shoebox works well), gluing them to Popsicle sticks, and holding them up between the light and the wall.

Fun Facts: No one really knows how long hand shadows have been around—probably since caveman days!

Jacks

(also called Dibs, Jackstones, Knucklebones, Onesies, and Snobs)

WHO: just you

WHAT YOU NEED: a flat surface, a set of jacks, a tiny rubber ball

OBJECT: See how many jacks you can pick up at one time.

Jacks is a very simple game, but since it's one of the world's oldest games, there are an almost endless number of variations.

To play the basic game, scatter the jacks on the ground. That means gently throwing them up in the air so that they fall and land at random—similar to how you would toss a pair of dice. Then throw the ball in the air. Using the same hand you used to throw the ball, pick up one of the jacks. Now catch the ball after it bounces once, but *before* it bounces twice, with that same hand, and the jack still *in* that hand. After you've caught the ball, you can transfer the jack to your other hand or set it aside while you continue playing.

Easy, huh? Well, maybe not. Depending on how simple or difficult you want things to be (or on how many come in the set you have!), you can play with five, ten, or fifteen jacks. Here's how the game progresses: The sequence for playing is the same, whether you stop at Fivesies or go all the way to Fifteensies. But be warned: Trying to pick up fifteen jacks at one time is a real challenge!

1. Onesies: Throw the ball, pick up one jack, catch the ball with the same hand. Move the jack to your other hand and go again. Repeat till you have picked up all the jacks. If you drop a jack or touch any jack other than the one you're trying to pick up, you have to start all over again. (Or if you're playing with partners, your turn ends.)

2. Twosies: Throw the ball, pick up two jacks at a time, catch the ball. Continue as above.

3. Threesies: Throw the ball, pick up three jacks at a time, catch the ball. Continue as above.

4. Foursies: Throw the ball, pick up four jacks at a time, catch the ball. Continue as above.

5. Fivesies: Throw the ball, pick up five jacks at a time, catch the ball. Continue as above.

Variations

- Today's jacks are usually made of metal or plastic, have six legs, and look like an asterisk or a star, but early jacks were usually made of stones or shells. For fun, you could hunt for some tiny, smooth pebbles and use those as your jacks.

- You can also play jacks with your friends. Have each person throw the jacks into the air; whoever catches the most goes first. If there's a tie, decide who goes first by "flipping," or catching the jacks on the back of your hand instead of in your palm (a lot harder to do!). That person plays until he fails to complete whatever sequence you decide to attempt. The first person to complete the sequence is the winner.

- Crack the Egg: Throw the ball in the air, pick up one jack and tap it on the ground, then catch the ball after it bounces once. Repeat until you have picked up all five (or more) jacks. Now play again, but this time tap each jack *twice* before catching the ball. Try to add one more tap to each round. The game ends if you drop any jacks or fail to catch the ball.

- Danger: Throw one jack into the air as you scoop up another, then catch the first on its way down. Then throw those two up in the air as you scoop up another, and catch the two you threw on their way down. Repeat the process until you are throwing all five jacks up in the air at the same time.

- Horses in the Stable: Make a "stable" out of your non-throwing hand by placing the tips of your fingers and thumb on the ground with your palm arched above them. Put a jack in each of the four "stalls" (the spaces between your fingers). Throw the ball up in the air, push one of the jacks, or "horses," into the stable, and catch the ball. Repeat until all the horses are in the stable, then throw the ball one last time as you scoop up all the horses.

- Pigs in the Pen: Make a "pigpen" by resting the side of your non-throwing hand on the ground and curving your fingers and thumb like the letter *C*. Throw the ball, push one of the jacks, or "pigs," into the pigpen, then catch the ball before it hits the ground. Repeat until you have pushed all the pigs into the pen.

- Sweep the Floor: Throw the ball up in the air and use your fingertips to "sweep" one jack next to another one, then catch the ball before it hits the ground. Repeat until all the jacks are swept together in a single cluster, then throw the ball one more time and pick up the entire cluster.

Fun Facts: Early jacks were often made from the backbone vertebrae, called knucklebones, of animals such as sheep or goats. Though the jacks themselves have changed over time, the game has been a constant for thousands of years. In Zimbabwe today, jacks is called Kudoda; in Israel, it's Kugelach; in England, Five Stones.

Juggling

WHO: just you

WHAT YOU NEED: 3 small rubber balls

OBJECT: Keep all three balls in the air at the same time without dropping them.

. . . .

While juggling looks difficult, it really isn't. As is the case with most new skills, it mostly requires concentration and practice.

Hold one ball in the palm of your dominant hand. With your elbows close to your sides and your arms extended in front of you at waist level, toss the ball up in an arc, to about eye level, then catch it with your other hand. Don't reach up for it; keep your catching hand at around waist height and let the ball come to you. As you catch the ball, let your hand sink a bit, gently cushioning its landing, then immediately propel it up into the arc again. Repeat this process until it feels comfortable and natural.

Now add a second ball. Put a ball in each hand, then toss the ball from your dominant hand in an arc toward your other hand. When that ball reaches the top of the arc and starts its descent, toss the ball from your

other hand toward your dominant hand, keeping the arc below that of the first ball. Ideally, the balls will land in your hands one after the other. Make sure you are throwing *both* balls up in the air, not just tossing the second one from one hand straight over to the other. You might try practicing in front of a mirror so you can see exactly what you're doing. Throwing one ball higher or adjusting your timing a bit could make things easier. Practice doing this two-ball routine until you feel comfortable and are catching the balls every time.

Add a third ball. Take a deep breath and remember that, most of the time, there's really only one ball in the air; good timing is the key to success. Hold two balls in your dominant hand and one in your other hand. Toss one of the balls in your dominant hand in a high arc toward the other hand. When the ball reaches the top of the arc and begins its descent, throw the ball from the other hand back toward your dominant hand. When that ball reaches the top of *its* arc and starts to come down, toss the third ball. Catch all the balls. You should have two balls in your nondominant hand and one in your dominant hand. Return one to your dominant hand and repeat the process over and over until you feel confident and are not dropping the balls. Then give yourself a big pat on the back: This is called a three-ball cascade, and you're now an official juggler!

Tips

- If you don't have three balls handy, you can use three of anything that is similar in size: oranges, beanbags, plastic eggs, etc. Three identical balls are probably easiest, though, because they're smooth, solid, and have the same weight.

- Standing in front of a wall in the early stages may help you focus and concentrate on the balls and not get distracted.

Fun Facts: Juggling is a *seriously* old game: Egyptians were tossing things in the air more than four thousand years ago—rings, balls, clubs, even swords and fiery torches! Early jugglers often did magic tricks or other forms of entertainment; today, we usually find jugglers in the circus. Maybe you can master juggling in time to celebrate World Juggling Day, held annually on the third Saturday in June.

Kite

WHO: just you

WHAT YOU NEED: a sheet of 8 1/2 x 11-inch paper, crayons or markers, an 8-inch bamboo skewer, clear tape, a plastic shopping bag, a ruler, a roll of kite string or other lightweight string, a hole punch

OBJECT: Create a kite that will float in the air when there's a breeze.

Use your crayons or markers to decorate both sides of the paper with a colorful design. Fold the paper in half so that it measures 8 1/2 x 5 1/2 inches. Use the edge of the ruler to firmly crease the fold. (Be sure your artwork is dry and be careful not to smudge it!) Unfold the paper and place it on a table in front of you like an open book.

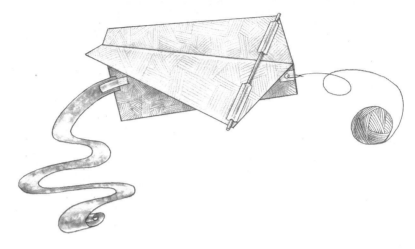

At the top of the page, make a mark 1 1/2 inches to the right of the crease and another 1 1/2 inches to the left of the crease. At the bottom of the page, make a mark 4 inches to the right of the crease and a mark 4 inches to the left of the crease. Using the ruler to keep it straight, draw a line from the top mark to the bottom mark on the right side of the page, then draw another line from the top mark to the bottom mark on the left side of the page.

Fold the paper in half again along the crease you made before so that the lines you drew are on the inside. Fold the top layer of the paper back toward you along the line you drew. Now flip over the paper and fold the other layer back toward you along the line.

Pick up the paper and hold it by the center crease, with the two folded "wings" sticking out to the side, as if it were a paper airplane. Lay the bamboo skewer across the wings between the two widest points and tape it into place securely. This will hold your wings in an upright position.

On the back vertical edge of the kite (the end farthest from the skewer), place a piece of tape about three or four inches long, from the wings to the bottom crease, so that the two sides of the kite are held together. Halfway between the wings and the crease, about an inch from the edge, use the hole punch to make a hole in the kite. Place tape over the front and back of the hole to reinforce it, then repunch the hole through the tape so the hole is not blocked. Thread the end of your ball of string through the hole and knot it securely. This string is how you'll control your kite once it's in the air; you will unroll it to let the kite fly higher and reroll to bring it back.

Make a tail for your kite by cutting a large plastic shopping bag into a 1-inch wide strip, starting at the open end of the bag and cutting in a spiral—like peeling an apple without breaking the peel. Your tail needs to be six to ten feet long. Tape the tail into place on the vertical edge under the skewered side of the wings, on the opposite end of the kite from where you tied the string.

Take your kite outside, wait for it to catch a breeze, quickly unroll your string, and let it soar!

Fun Facts: People have been flying kites for two thousand years. They are especially popular in China and Japan. Kites have also been used for military action, scientific research, sporting events, and even transportation.

O'Leary

WHO: 1 player

WHAT YOU NEED: a small rubber ball or tennis ball

OBJECT: Bounce and catch the ball at the appropriate time.

Recite this rhyme, bouncing the ball on "one, two, three" (or the other numbers at the beginning of the line), then pass your leg over the ball when you say "O'Leary," and catch the ball when it rebounds.

> One, two, three, O'Leary,
> Four, five, six, O'Leary,
> Seven, eight, nine, O'Leary,
> Ten O'Leary, catch me!

Variations

• Bounce the ball off a wall instead of the floor.

• Clap your hands after you bounce the ball and say "O'Leary."

• Do a 360-degree spin after you bounce the ball and say "O'Leary."

• Cross your hands in front of you after you bounce the ball and say "O'Leary."

• Sing the O'Leary rhyme to the tune of "Ten Little Indians."

• Do this sequence of actions:

> One: Bounce the ball off a wall under your raised right leg, then catch it.
> Two: Bounce the ball off a wall under your raised left leg, then catch it.
> Three: Bounce the ball off the ground and catch it under your raised right leg.
> O'Leary: Bounce the ball off the ground and catch it.
> Four: Bounce the ball off the ground and catch it under your raised left leg.
> Five: Bounce the ball off a wall and catch it in the air on a circle made by joining your right thumb and index finger at their tips.

Six: Bounce the ball off a wall and catch it in the air on a circle made by joining your left thumb and index finger at their tips.

O'Leary: Bounce the ball off the ground and catch it.

Seven: Throw the ball against a wall, twirl around once to the right, and catch the ball.

Eight: Throw the ball against a wall, twirl around once to the left, and catch the ball.

Nine: Bounce the ball off the ground, bend your knees and touch both hands to the ground, stand back up, and catch the ball.

O'Leary: Bounce the ball off the ground and catch it.

Catch me!

Oliver Twist

WHO: 1 or more players

WHAT YOU NEED: a small rubber ball

OBJECT: Bounce a ball off a wall while reciting a rhyme and do different actions before catching it again.

. . . .

Say the rhyme below while bouncing the ball off a wall. While the ball is bouncing, do the action listed next to the rhyme's text, finishing it before catching the ball with either hand. If you drop the ball or make a mistake with the rhyme or the action, you have to start again from the beginning. (Or, if you're playing with partners, it becomes the next person's turn.) If you get all the way through the rhyme, you get to repeat it—but this time you have to catch the ball with only your right hand. The next time you get all the way through the rhyme and start again, use only your left hand.

The Rhyme

Oliver Twist, *(bounce, catch)*
Can you do this? *(bounce, catch)*
If so, *(bounce, catch)*
Do so. *(bounce, catch)*
Number one, *(bounce, catch)*
Touch your tongue. *(bounce, touch tongue, catch)*
Number two, *(bounce, catch)*

Touch your shoe. (*bounce, touch shoe, catch*)

Number three, (*bounce, catch*)

Touch your knee. (*bounce, touch knee, catch*)

Number four, (*bounce, catch*)

Touch the floor. (*bounce, touch ground, catch*)

Number five, (*bounce, catch*)

Make a hive. (*bounce, crouch with hands touching overhead, catch*)

Number six, (*bounce, catch*)

Touch the bricks. (*bounce, touch wall, catch*)

Number seven, (*bounce, catch*)

Go to heaven. (*bounce, jump in the air with your arms raised, catch*)

Number eight, (*bounce, catch*)

Touch your mate. (*bounce, touch the person next to you or your own shoulder if you're playing alone, catch*)

Number nine, (*bounce, catch*)

Touch your spine. (*bounce, touch your spine, catch*)

Number ten, (*bounce, catch*)

Start again. (*bounce, catch, and start again*)

Tips

- First, practice throwing and catching the ball in time with the words, without trying to do any actions.

- Release the ball to match the rhythm of the words, throwing or bouncing on the emphasized (usually the first) word: "*Oliver* Twist, can *you* do this? *If* so, *do* so," etc.

Variations

- Bounce the ball on the floor instead of off the wall.

- Play with two or more players and take turns when one of you messes up.

Parachute

WHO: just you

WHAT YOU NEED: plastic shopping bag, string, plastic figure (like a toy soldier), a hole punch, tape

OBJECT: Make a parachute that will fly through the sky.

Cut the shopping bag up one side and across the bottom, and spread it out flat. Cut out a square from the bag—however small or large you want it to be. (You can use a ruler to measure and get it exactly square, or you can just eyeball it.) Use the hole punch to make a hole in each corner of the square. Make sure the hole is at least 1/2 inch from the edge to prevent tearing. Place tape over the front and back of the hole to reinforce it, then repunch the hole through the tape so the hole is not blocked.

Cut four pieces of string, each one 24 inches long. Tie one end of each string to one of the four corners of the plastic square. Tie the other ends of the strings to the plastic figure. Hold the plastic figure in one hand and use the other hand to gather up the plastic square. Hold the gathered-up plastic square on top of the plastic figure and throw them up into the air. Your parachute and figure should float down from the sky.

Variations

• If you have a friend visiting, make two parachutes and let them race to see whose hits the ground first. Or one of you drop the parachute from a high spot, such as a deck or the top of a slide, while the other person tries to catch it down below.

Rocket Ball

WHO: just you

WHAT YOU NEED: a tennis ball or small rubber ball, knee-high panty hose or sock

OBJECT: Send the ball hurtling into the air, then catch it.

Place the ball in the toe of the stocking, then knot the stocking just above the ball to keep it in place. Hold the end of the stocking, swing it around several times, then release it into the air. Run and try to catch it before it hits the ground.

Variations

• Swing the ball against a wall and catch it on the rebound.

• Turn this into a fun activity for several friends by tying lots of rocket balls together: Tie the loose end of the stocking around the next rocket ball's toe (with the ball in it). Then have one person swing the long string of rocket balls around while everyone else leaps over it.

Shoot 'Em Out

WHO: just you

WHAT YOU NEED: candles, matches, a squirt gun, a bucket of water, putty or candlesticks to keep candles in place, a fence or table or tree stump to put candles on

OBJECT: Shoot out the candle flames with a squirt gun.

Ask a grown-up to help you with the candles and matches in this game. Also, do not play this inside, on windy days, or in an area with dry grass or foliage.

Set up candles in a row outside on a fence, table, or tree stump. Fill up a squirt gun with water. Have a grown-up help you light the candles. Stand a good distance away from the candles (ten to twenty feet is good) and try to extinguish the flames with your squirt gun.

Tips

- Only children who are old enough to know and practice fire safety should play this game.

- You might want to keep some spare candles handy, since wicks can be hard to relight after they get wet.

- Short, fat candles are easier to work with than tall, skinny ones.

- Play this with others as a relay race or a skill game.

Shuttlecock

WHO: just you

WHAT YOU NEED: a wine cork, 20 feathers of about the same size

OBJECT: See if you can get the shuttlecock to spin through the air.

Stick the quill end of the feathers into the smaller end of the wine cork, twisting and arranging them to create a nice, full circle. Throw your shuttlecock up in the air; it should spiral downward and land on the featherless end.

Tips

- If the feathers won't go deep enough into the cork to stay in place, ask an adult to use a knife or a pin to help make deeper holes.

- If the feathers fall out, dip the ends in a little glue, then stick them back into the cork.

Variations

- You can use the heel and toe of your foot to kick the shuttlecock up in the air and try to keep it from hitting the ground for as long as possible.

Stone Skipping

(also called Ducks and Drakes, Ricochet, and Stone Skiffing)

WHO: just you

WHAT YOU NEED: small, flat stones; a body of water

OBJECT: See how many times you can get the stone to skip across the water.

Hold a stone in your throwing hand so that it fits snugly in the curve between your thumb and index finger, with your other fingers tucked underneath. Put the flattest side facing down. There are two ways you can throw: across your body or from behind your body.

To throw across your body, turn so that your throwing arm is closest to the water. If you're left-handed, the water should be on your left; if you're right-handed, it should be on your right. Take a deep breath and bend your knees slightly as you bring your throwing arm toward your body (as if you're going to hug yourself), then fling it out toward the water as you release the stone.

To throw from behind your body, turn so that your throwing arm is farther from the water. If you're left-handed, the water should be on your right; if you're right-handed, it should be on your left. Take a deep breath and bend your knees slightly as you pull your throwing arm back away from the water, then fling it out toward the water as you release the stone.

Tips

- Stones that are small (2–3 inches in diameter is perfect), round, and smooth make the best skippers.

- Stones that are really light or really heavy for their size don't skip as well.

- Try to throw the stone straight out at the water level, not up toward the sky or down into the water. For you math lovers, an angle of 20 degrees is considered ideal.

- If the stone hits the water and then bounces really high into the air, try to make it land farther away from you the next time so the angle is not so steep.

Fun Facts: People have been skipping stones since the days of the ancient Greeks. The current world record was set by Russell Byars of Franklin, Pennsylvania, on July 19, 2007, with a whopping fifty-one skips!

String Games

WHO: just you

WHAT YOU NEED: a piece of string or yarn as long as you are tall

OBJECT: Make a variety of shapes and patterns with your fingers and a piece of string.

Playing string games is a lot of fun, and because all it requires is a piece of string, you can entertain yourself (and others!) almost any time or any place. Stuck going to the grocery store or hardware store with your mom or dad? Keep a piece of string in your pocket and you'll never be bored again!

The usual recommendation for string length is six feet, so that when you tie the ends together you get a three-foot loop. However, to make sure the string is a comfortable length for you to handle, a better idea is to hold the end of the string in one hand, hold that hand straight up over your head, then have someone cut the string right where it hits the ground. Tie the two ends together and you'll have a string that's just the right size for *you.*

The Smile

Hold either end of your string loop in your hands. Stretch it out, then let the loop droop in the center so that it forms a smile.

Thumb Trap

Hold your hands in front of you with the palms facing each other. Put the string behind the thumbs and little fingers of both hands and pull the strings taut. (This is called Position 1, and you will use it often in string games.) Twist the loop to create an X in the center by switching the position of the string on one hand.

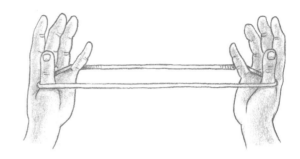

Now lift the string sitting on your left palm with your right index finger, creating a new loop around that finger. With your left index finger, lift the right palm string from inside the new loop you just made. Insert your thumbs into the forefinger loops.

Keeping the string on your thumbs, bend your hands inward, letting the strings fall off your index and little fingers of both hands. Pull your hands apart as far as they will go and you'll find that your thumbs are trapped!

Cup and Saucer

Hold your hands in front of you with the palms facing each other. Put the string behind the thumbs and little fingers of both hands and pull the strings taut (Position 1). Lift the string sitting on your left palm with your right index finger, creating a new loop around that finger. With your left index finger, lift the right palm string from inside the new loop you just made, and pull the strings taut. It should look like the image on the right.

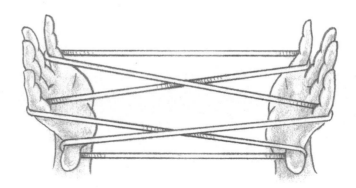

Bend your thumbs *over* the near forefinger strings, then pick up the *far* forefinger strings with both thumbs. Using fingers from the opposite hand, and being careful not to lose any strings, lift the lower thumb string up and over both thumbs, while leaving the upper strings in place. Release both your little fingers as you pull outward with your thumbs. Position your hands so that your thumbs are on top. It should look like this; can you see the cup and saucer?

Star

Double your string so your loop is half the size. Hold your hands in front of you with the palms facing each other. Put the string behind the thumbs and little fingers of both hands and pull the strings taut (Position 1). You'll have two rows of string around your thumbs and pinkies instead of one.

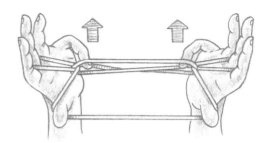

Follow the instructions above to make a Cup and Saucer. Flip your hands so that your thumbs are pointing toward your face. In the middle of the figure, where the bottom of the cup sits on the saucer, you'll see three strings: Two are crossed and go to the near side of the forefingers, and the other is below them and loops around the far forefinger and far thumb strings. Use your pinkies to pick up the bottom string as shown.

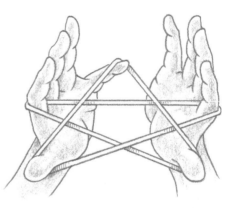

Release the strings on your thumbs. Move your thumbs over the forefinger loops and pick up the nearest pinky strings. Release *only* the string loop on your right pinky. It should look like the image on the right.

Fun Facts: String games have been played since the Stone Age. There's evidence of them in almost every part of the world. In some cultures, a long, thin strand of animal skin was used instead of string; in others, they used a weave of human hair. In the Pacific Islands, they made string from plant fibers. Sometimes, storytellers used string figures to help tell their stories. If you enjoy these string games, the International String Figure Association website offers a new string figure design every month. For more information, go to www.isfa.org/sfotm/sfotm_2011.htm.

Whirly Cob

WHO: just you

WHAT YOU NEED: a corn cob, 2 long feathers

OBJECT: See how far and how fast you can get the whirly cob to go.

Rinse a corn cob from which all the kernels have been eaten or otherwise removed. Break it in half so that the soft center is exposed. Stick the quill end of the feathers into the soft center. When you throw the cob, it will twist and whirl through the air.

Yo-Yo
(also called Bandelure and Quiz)

WHO: just you

WHAT YOU NEED: a yo-yo

OBJECT: Have fun!

Yo-yo toys have been around since the days of ancient Greece and, possibly, ancient China. As they've developed over the centuries, yo-yos have been made from clay, wood, metal, and plastic. Their design relies on a mix of gravity, timing, and agility to entertain both practitioner and spectator. A good quality yo-yo will perform and hold up better, so don't buy the cheapest one you see. A slip-string yo-yo is a good choice for beginners who want to learn the basic tricks that follow.

Getting Started

Make sure your yo-yo string is untangled by holding the top of the string and letting the yo-yo dangle freely at the end. If the string reaches past your waist when the yo-yo is sitting on the ground, you may need to shorten it. Just cut off the excess and create a new loop at the top. Instead of putting that loop over your middle finger, push the string *through* the loop to create a slipknot. *That's* what goes on your finger.

To wind up the yo-yo, wrap your hand around it, with your fingers right at the edge of one of the two halves. Wrap the string around the yo-yo and your forefinger the first time, then lift your finger (with the string still on it) and wrap the string around two more times. Now take your finger out from underneath the string, tuck the loop between the two halves, and finish wrapping the string around the yo-yo. Slide the slipknot onto your middle finger and let the yo-yo go down and up one time. You should be ready to go.

Here are some basic yo-yo moves and tricks. If you have a hard time, just keep practicing; the secret to getting good is repetition!

Gravity Pull

Hold the yo-yo in front of you in your dominant hand with the palm down, just above your waist. Loop the slipknot over your middle finger and close your hand around the yo-yo. Open your hand and let the yo-yo unroll toward the ground. At the exact second that the yo-yo gets to the end of its string near the ground, jerk your hand upward. The yo-yo will wind up and come back into your hand.

Throw Down

Hold your yo-yo-throwing hand out in front of you at shoulder level with the palm up. Loop the slipknot over your middle finger, then use your thumb and middle finger to make the yo-yo balance on its edge in your palm. The string should be positioned to come off from the top and front of the yo-yo (closer to your fingers than your wrist).

Still holding the yo-yo between your thumb and middle finger, bend your elbow to bring your hand to your shoulder. Then quickly straighten your elbow and fling the yo-yo away from you as you let go of it, your hand twisting to face down. When the yo-yo reaches the end of the string near the ground, quickly pull your arm upward slightly and the yo-yo should start climbing back up the string.

The Sleeper

Hold your yo-yo-throwing hand out in front of you, at shoulder level, with the palm up. Loop the slipknot over your middle finger, then use your thumb and middle finger to make the yo-yo balance on its edge in your palm. The string should be positioned to come off from the top and front of the yo-yo (closer to your fingers than your wrist).

Hold on to the yo-yo as you bend your elbow to bring your hand to your shoulder. Then quickly straighten your elbow and fling the yo-yo away from you as you let go of it, your hand twisting to face down. The yo-yo should immediately travel down the string and, if the tension is correct, the yo-yo should spin at the end of the string, or "sleep," for a few seconds.

Before it stops spinning, jerk your hand upward and the yo-yo should come back up the string into your hand. If the yo-yo continues to hang and spin, the string is too loose. Tighten it by letting the yo-yo dangle at the end of the string until it's still, then spin the yo-yo clockwise for a few seconds before rewinding it. If the yo-yo doesn't spin at all when you throw it down, but comes right back up to your hand, the string is wound too tightly. Loosen it by dangling the yo-yo at the end of the string and twisting it in a counterclockwise direction.

Forward Pass

Hold your yo-yo in your hand with the slipknot looped over your middle finger, your arm down at your side, the palm of your hand facing behind you, and your thumb and middle finger holding the yo-yo in your palm. Swing your wrist and arm up and forward, throwing the yo-yo directly out in front of you. When the yo-yo gets to the end of the string, turn your hand so that your palm is facing up, jerk your hand back slightly to start the yo-yo back up the string, then catch it in your palm.

After you've mastered these basic yo-yo techniques, you might want to try the tricks on the following pages. Don't get discouraged if you can't do them right away. Just keep practicing!

Around the World

Stand someplace where you have plenty of room (at least ten feet in all directions, including over your head). Make sure there are no people, animals, or breakable objects within the area.

Hold your yo-yo in your hand with the slipknot looped over your middle finger, your arm down at your side, the palm of your hand facing behind you, and your thumb and middle finger holding the yo-yo in your palm.

Swing your wrist and arm up and forward, throwing the yo-yo directly out in front of you. When the yo-yo reaches the end of its string, with your hand held at waist level, swing the yo-yo over your shoulder and behind you in a 360-degree circle. The yo-yo should remain at the end of the string throughout the whole trick, spinning as it makes the circle beside your body. When the yo-yo has made one complete circle, jerk your hand so the yo-yo can come up the string and return to your hand.

Pinwheel

Hold your yo-yo-throwing hand out in front of you, at shoulder level, with the palm up. Loop the slipknot over your middle finger, then use your thumb and middle finger to make the yo-yo balance on its edge in your palm. The string should be positioned to come off from the top and front of the yo-yo (closer to your fingers than your wrist).

Hold on to the yo-yo as you bend your elbow to bring your hand to your shoulder. Then quickly straighten your elbow and fling the yo-yo away from you as you let go of it, your hand twisting to face down. The yo-yo should immediately travel down the string and, if the tension is correct, the yo-yo should spin at the end of the string.

With the thumb and middle finger of your non-throwing hand, grab the string about two-thirds of the way down. Move that hand up and sideways as you move your yo-yo hand down, so that your two hands are almost the same level in front of you, with the yo-yo hanging from your free hand.

Use the wrist of your free hand to make the yo-yo swing in a circle, or a "pinwheel," several times. To end the trick, throw the yo-yo forward as you release the string and let the yo-yo climb back up to your hand.

Rock the Baby

Hold your yo-yo-throwing hand out in front of you, at shoulder level, with the palm up. Loop the slipknot over your middle finger, then use your thumb and middle finger to make the yo-yo balance on its edge in your palm. The string should be positioned to come off from the top and front of the yo-yo (closer to your fingers than your wrist).

Hold on to the yo-yo as you bend your elbow to bring your hand to your shoulder. Then quickly straighten your elbow and fling the yo-yo away from you as you let go of it, your hand twisting to face down. The yo-yo should immediately travel down the string and, if the tension is correct, the yo-yo should spin at the end of the string.

Lift up your yo-yo hand until it is slightly higher than your head. Hold out your other hand about a third of the way down the string, with the palm facing down. Bring your yo-yo hand down and over the non-throwing hand, draping the string over your fingers.

Now grab the string a few inches above the yo-yo with your yo-yo hand. As you bring your yo-yo hand up above your non-throwing hand, turn your non-throwing palm faceup and lower it slightly. If you've done this correctly, your yo-yo will be rocking back and forth in the middle of a triangle, or "cradle," that you've created. To end this trick, jerk your yo-yo hand and let go of the string with your non-throwing hand, and the yo-yo should climb up the string and return to your hand.

Walk the Dog

Hold your yo-yo-throwing hand out in front of you, at shoulder level, with the palm up. Loop the slipknot over your middle finger, then use your thumb and middle finger to make the yo-yo balance on its edge in your palm. The string should be positioned to come off from the top and front of the yo-yo (closer to your fingers than your wrist).

Hold on to the yo-yo as you bend your elbow to bring your hand to your shoulder. Then quickly straighten your elbow and fling the yo-yo away from you as you let go of it, your hand twisting to face down. The yo-yo should immediately travel down the string and, if the tension is correct, the yo-yo should spin at the end of the string.

Swing the yo-yo slightly forward and, very gently, let it rest on the ground. (Smooth surfaces work best, such as firm carpet or tile flooring; rough surfaces like cement can scratch your yo-yo and interfere with its performance, and very soft surfaces like plush carpet can slow down the spin too much.) The spin of the yo-yo will make it roll forward along the ground. Before the yo-yo stops spinning, give your hand a slight jerk so it will return to your hand.

Fun Facts: Yo-yo is the Filipino word for *come back.*

The Duncan Toys Company, the American manufacturer that made *yo-yo* a household word, sold forty-five million *yo-yos* at the peak of the toy's popularity in 1962. Donald Duncan didn't actually invent the yo-yo (various forms of this toy have been around since about 500 BC!), but he *did* invent the Eskimo Pie and Good Humor ice cream bars.

The National Yo-Yo Museum is located in Chico, California, and sponsors a yo-yo contest every year on the first Saturday of October. The museum offers free yo-yo lessons every Saturday from noon until two P.M.

A Is for Armadillo

Players must spot and name three objects that start with A, then B, then C. Play continues all the way to the end of the alphabet. Only one player is allowed to use a specific object. For example, for B, if someone says, "This bridge!" referring to a bridge the car is currently traveling over, no other player can claim that bridge as their B. Five miles down the road, however, another bridge is fair game for another player. Whoever gets to Z first is the winner.

Variations

• Pick a letter of the alphabet. Whoever spots the most objects beginning with that letter within a certain period of time wins and gets to choose the next letter.

• The first person says, "A is for *alphabet*"; the next person says, "A is for *alphabet*, B is for *birdbrains*"; the next person says, "A is for *alphabet*, B is for *birdbrains*, C is for *crayons*"; and play continues until you work your way through the entire alphabet.

Alphabet Game

Everyone begins at the same time, first trying to spot an *A* on a street sign, billboard, building, license plate, etc. When they spot it, they call out where they found it. For example, "*A* on that billboard for Fatt Matt's Barbecue!" No other person may then claim that location for a letter. Play progresses with each person keeping track of their own letters and calling them out as you travel down the road.

Variations

- Instead of competing for letters individually, you can work together and take turns, with the first person looking for an *A*, the second person looking for a *B*, and so forth.

- If the area in which you're traveling doesn't have much signage, you can choose a theme (foods, cities, animals, etc.), start with the letter *A*, and have people take turns calling out things that begin with that letter. For example, if your theme is clothing and the letter is *A*, possible words might be *apron*, *ascot*, and *angora sweater*. Change to the next letter when everyone has had a turn or when you run out of ideas for that letter.

Fun Facts: Reading roadside signs was especially fun from the 1930s through the 1950s, when companies such as Burma-Shave and Rock City Gardens had nationwide advertising campaigns that centered around repetitive, recognizable road signs. Burma-Shave's technique was to stagger four or five short, funny sentence fragments one after another on the roadside so that people kept watching to read the entire sentence. For example: "Don't stick / Your elbow / Out so far / It might go home / In another car / Burma-Shave." Rock City's gimmick was to paint "See Rock City" on barns across the United States, encouraging families to come visit Lover's Leap and the Swing-A-Long Bridge, and to see the lavish gardens and "seven states from 1,700 feet above sea level!" While Rock City is still alive and well, only about a hundred remain of the nine hundred barns that once beckoned travelers across America to Lookout Mountain, Georgia.

Bridges and Tunnels

WHO: whoever's in the car and wants to play

WHAT YOU NEED: good lungs

OBJECT: Hold your breath until you get all the way across a bridge or through a tunnel.

. . . .

This game's pretty simple, but it can make a dull ride a little more interesting. Every time you go through a tunnel or pass over a bridge, have everyone take a deep breath and see if they can hold their breath until you get all the way through the tunnel or all the way over the bridge.

Fun Facts: The longest undersea tunnel in the world is the Seikan Tunnel in Japan, which connects the islands of Hokkaido and Honshu. It is 33.46 miles long. (Don't try to hold your breath in *that* one!)

Buzz

WHO: whoever's in the car and wants to play

WHAT YOU NEED: your thinking cap

OBJECT: Count to 100, replacing any number divisible by 7 with the word *buzz.*

. . . .

This game's not hard, but you have to pay attention. Take turns, with every person saying a number as you count from one to one hundred. Anyone whose number is divisible by seven, or that has a seven in it, must say "Buzz!" instead of the number. For example: 1, 2, 3, 4, 5, 6, BUZZ!, 8, 9, 10, 11, 12, 13, BUZZ!, 15, 16, BUZZ!, etc. If you forget and say the number instead of "Buzz!" you're out of the game. The last person remaining in the game is the winner.

Counting Cows
(also called Cow Poker)

WHO: whoever's in the car and wants to play

WHAT YOU NEED: good eyes

OBJECT: Help your team count the most cows.

Divide the occupants of your car into two teams: People on the left will claim cows on the left side of the road, and people on the right will claim cows on the right side of the road. (People in the middle will have to choose one or the other!) Decide on a time limit—thirty minutes, till you stop for lunch, the length of your trip, etc. Each team counts any cows spotted on their side of the road. Work together as a team for a collective count; you might spot a cow that Mom missed, but that's a point for the whole team, not just you. You'll have to decide up front if points will be given for cow statues, cow billboards, etc., or just *live* cows.

If there's a graveyard on your side of the road and someone from the other team sees it and says, "Your cows are buried!" you lose *all* your cow points. If nobody from the other team notices the graveyard . . . well . . . just keep on counting! It's perfectly legal to distract your opponents if you see a cemetery coming up on *your* side of the road . . . or a whole lot of cows on *theirs*!

Variations

- Traditionally, spotting a white horse is worth fifty extra points, but you can create whatever "bonus point" challenges you'd like. For example, a bull with horns could be worth an extra fifty points, or a calf could be worth one hundred points.

- Count other things besides cows. Horses, dogs, RVs, barns . . . whatever seems fun!

- A similar game is Birds on a Wire: Divide into teams and watch for birds sitting on telephone wires on either side of the road. Whoever gets to a certain number first wins. Only birds that are *on* the wire count; if one flies away while you're counting, there goes a point!

Dots and Boxes

(also called Boxes, Dots, Dot Boxing, and Square-it)

WHO: anybody in the car who's not driving

WHAT YOU NEED: a piece of paper, a pen or pencil

OBJECT: Draw the most boxes.

This is a great car game because it can be as long or as short as you'd like.

On a sheet of paper, make straight rows of dots down and across, about 1/2 inch to 1 inch apart. The first player draws a vertical or horizontal line from one dot to another immediately next to it, either up/down or across. The next player does the same thing. Play continues until everyone has had a turn, then it's the first player's turn again. He draws another line, either continuing where he left off or anywhere else he likes. When a player forms a complete box, she writes her initial inside the box and gets to take another turn. The player with the most boxes when you can make no more lines, or decide to end the game, wins.

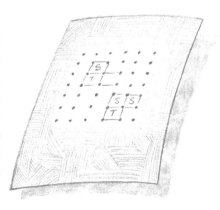

Find 100

WHO: whoever's in the car and wants to play

WHAT YOU NEED: good eyes, your thinking cap

OBJECT: Spot 100 of whatever you're counting.

Each player chooses an object or color, and then counts those objects or objects of that color until they find one hundred of them. You might choose green cars, horse trailers, brown cows, statues, red convertibles, blonde women, or motorcycles. Whoever spots their one hundred items first is the winner.

Highway Scavenger Hunt

WHO: anybody in the car who's not driving

WHAT YOU NEED: a list of things to find for every player, a pencil or marker

OBJECT: Be the first person to find all the things on the list.

Have you ever been on a scavenger hunt? They're great fun! Someone (usually your mom or dad) puts together a random list of items, and players take off exploring in all directions to bring the items back. With the advent of cell phone cameras, now instead of bringing back the actual items, players often just take pictures of them instead.

A highway scavenger hunt is only a little different. Instead of going out to find items or taking pictures of them, you simply spot them as you ride down the road and check them off your list. If you like, you can play on teams instead of as individuals. Ready, set, scavenge!

Only one person can claim an object. Whoever spots an ice-cream cone (marching band, cement truck, policeman, etc.) first gets to claim it. Everyone else will have to wait for the *next* ice-cream cone (or other item) to come along!

Make sure your list of objects is appropriate for the route you're taking. For example, if you're driving from Indiana to Texas, you are *not* going to find any oceans, and if you're driving on a country back road through the beautiful Blue Ridge Mountains, there's not a skyscraper to be had. The first person to find all the objects listed wins the game.

Fun Facts: American author Elsa Maxwell is credited with inventing the scavenger hunt as a way to entertain her party guests during the 1930s.

License Plate Game

WHO: whoever's in the car and wants to play

WHAT YOU NEED: good eyes, a list of the 50 US states or a map of the United States

OBJECT: Try to spot license plates from all 50 US states.

This game works best on long trips when you're traveling through several states or are on the road for several days. It's also a fun game to play as a family, rather than as individuals.

Make a copy of the list on the next page. Pay attention to vehicles' license plates as they pass by, and check off all the different states you see. (If you use a map, make an X through a state when you spot a license plate from there.) Though you're limited to pure luck as to who drives past you on the highway, it's fun to try to get all the way to fifty.

To add some more fun, when you spot a state other than your own, see if anyone has a story about that state or knows anything special about it. For example, did you know that New Mexico has more sheep and cattle than people? Or that Rollerblades were invented by two Minnesota students who wanted to practice hockey off-season?

List of States

Alabama	Maine	Oregon
Alaska	Maryland	Pennsylvania
Arizona	Massachusetts	Rhode Island
Arkansas	Michigan	South Carolina
California	Minnesota	South Dakota
Colorado	Mississippi	Tennessee
Connecticut	Missouri	Texas
Delaware	Montana	Utah
Florida	Nebraska	Vermont
Georgia	Nevada	Virginia
Hawaii	New Hampshire	Washington
Idaho	New Jersey	West Virginia
Illinois	New Mexico	Wisconsin
Indiana	New York	Wyoming
Iowa	North Carolina	
Kansas	North Dakota	
Kentucky	Ohio	
Louisiana	Oklahoma	

License Plate Lingo

WHO: whoever's in the car and wants to play

WHAT YOU NEED: good eyes, a good imagination

OBJECT: Use license plate letters to create a phrase.

You know how most license plates contain a mix of letters and numbers? Well, the goal of this game is to use the letters to inspire a phrase or sentence that makes at least a *little* sense. For example, if the license plate of the Ford F-150 pickup that just passed you says "853-RBJ," you might call out, "Randy burped jelly," or "Really bad jackhammer." You have to use the letters in the order they appear on the license plate; no cheating! After you announce your phrase, the next player gets to pick out a license plate and do the same thing.

Variations

- Pick a license plate and then let everyone try to come up with a phrase for those letters before you pick another one.

Fun Facts: The first state-issued license plates were issued in Massachusetts in 1903.

Musical Miles

WHO: whoever's in the car and wants to play

WHAT YOU NEED: a radio, CD player, or MP3 player

OBJECT: Make a joyful noise.

Car time is a fantastic place to enjoy family time, be silly, and try things you might not usually do (like sing!). Have everyone bring along a favorite CD or tune in to a radio station that's playing great music and engage in a songfest. Solos, duets, four-part harmony . . . you might surprise yourself by how good you sound! Even if you and your parents or siblings don't usually like the same kind of music, there's probably an old

hymn that your grandmother taught to all of you, or a rock classic you all know and love. When all else fails, there's always "Bohemian Rhapsody," "The Lion Sleeps Tonight," "Old McDonald Had a Farm," and "99 Bottles of Beer on the Wall" to make those miles move along.

Fun Facts: "The Lion Sleeps Tonight" has been recorded by some forty different artists since the song was written in the 1920s by South African singer Solomon Linda. The original title was "Mbube," the Zulu word for *lion*.

Name That Tune

WHO: whoever's in the car and wants to play

WHAT YOU NEED: good ears

OBJECT: Be the first to guess what song someone is humming.

. . . .

The only rule for this game is that, to be fair, you should try to stick to songs you think everyone in the car will know. (No fair stumping Grandma with Justin Bieber's "Baby.") Choose a player to start. That person thinks of a song and hums the first note. (Players could also sing *la* instead of humming.) All the other players try to guess the song—which isn't likely to happen with just one note revealed. The singer continues to reveal one more note at a time until someone guesses the song. (Surprisingly, a lot of songs will be familiar after only four or five notes!) Whoever guesses the song gets to choose the next one.

Fun Facts: Name That Tune was actually a popular TV game show that aired during the 1950s, and again in the 1970s and 1980s. Players competed for a top prize of $100,000.

Punch Buggy
(also called Slug Bug)

WHO: anybody in the car who's not driving

WHAT YOU NEED: good eyes

OBJECT: Be the first player to spot a Volkswagen Beetle.

. . . .

Thanks to this game, several generations of children have grown up associating Volkswagens with getting punched in the arm! You might prefer to focus on points instead of punches; regular VW Beetles earn 1 point, VW convertibles earn 2 points. If you do decide to stick to the traditional game, please remember to punch gently.

The first player to spot a VW Beetle, or Bug, as they're also fondly known, punches (gently, please!) everyone around her in the biceps (upper arm) only, calls out "Punch Buggy!" and gets a point. If you yell "Punch Buggy!" and the car *isn't* a VW Beetle, you lose a point. And if you punch someone before you realize you made a mistake, either they get to punch *you* or you lose the opportunity to punch them the next time you get a point.

You can only claim the same vehicle one time. For example, if you spot a Beetle leaving a rest stop and claim a point, you can't claim another one when it passes you on the road five minutes later. (No one else can claim it, either.) If you happen to drive past a Volkswagen dealership, you are not allowed to claim any of the cars sitting on the lot. Should someone drive a Beetle off the lot and into the street while you happen to be watching, you *can* claim that one.

Variations

- Instead of just saying "Punch Buggy!" you can call out "Punch Buggy! No punch backs!" which means that no one can punch you back. If the claimant forgets to say "No punch backs!" the person she punched gets to (gently!) punch her back. If she *does* say "No punch backs!" and someone punches her back *anyway*, she gets to punch that person again.

- Specify the color of the car. For example, call out, "Red (green, blue, etc.) Punch Buggy!"

- Some people also give 2 points for VW vans.

- *Punch Buggy* seems to be primarily an East Coast term. Many people prefer the term *Slug Bug* and call out, "Slug Bug! No returns!"

- You can forget punches and points and just yell "Beetle Bop!" whenever you see a Bug.

- In Europe, a game is played that is similar to this one. Players call out "Yellow car" whenever they see a yellow car and follow it up with a punch.

- At night, when you can't tell if a car is a Punch Buggy or not, you can switch to a game called Popeye. If you spot a car with only one headlight, you can call "Popeye!" and get a point. Be careful, though; if it turns out to be a motorcycle, you lose your point.

Fun Facts: Nobody knows when or how the game of Punch Buggy really originated, but it was probably in the 1960s, when Beetles were really popular. That popularity came, in part, from the Disney movies that featured Herbie, the "Love Bug."

Road Trip Bingo

WHO: anybody in the car who's not driving

WHAT YOU NEED: a bingo card for every player, pencils or markers

OBJECT: Be the first player to spot five things in a row.

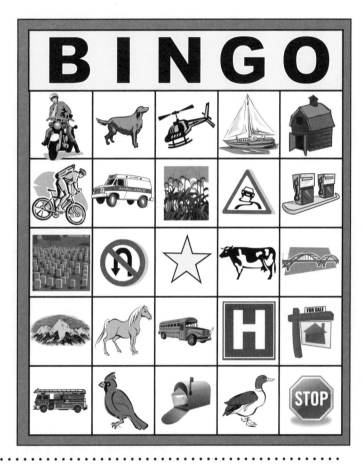

This game is played almost exactly like regular bingo, except instead of someone calling out numbers to everyone who's playing, everyone looks for the items on the bingo card as you drive down the road. Make this game more fun by creating "official" bingo cards before you start your trip. You can copy the design on the right or make up your own. If you like, you can just write words instead of drawing or cutting out pictures. The first player to spot a whole row of objects on their card—either vertically, horizontally, or diagonally—wins the game.

Variations

- Make the game simpler by using a grid of only nine objects instead of twenty-five. Don't forget your Free Spot in the center!

Fun Facts: Bingo was invented in Italy in the 1500s. Originally called Beano (because players marked their card squares with beans), the name changed when a player's tongue got twisted when announcing his win. It's been Bingo ever since!

The Car Next Door

WHO: whoever's in the car and wants to play

WHAT YOU NEED: your imagination

OBJECT: Make up the best story.

. . . .

This game is a lot of fun and can go on for hours as long as you can see inside the vehicles around you. Simply take a look inside the cars, trucks, and vans that you pass on the road and come up with a story about who they are and what they're doing. You can use visual clues to help create your story, or just make up details as you go along. For example, if your story is about the man in the pickup who just passed you, you might involve the German shepherd in the passenger seat, the lawn mower in the back of the truck, or the bumper sticker that says IF IT AIN'T BROKE, DON'T FIX IT! in your story. If it's dark and you can't see any passersby to inspire a story, think about what *your* family looks like as you're driving along, and make up a story about yourselves!

Tips

. . . .

• Be respectful. Don't stare or point at people as you observe them.

• If you like your story, write it down. You might be able to use it as the basis for a school assignment.

The Quiet Game

WHO: whoever's in the car and wants to play

WHAT YOU NEED: strong willpower

OBJECT: Be the quietest person in the car.

This is usually a *parent's* favorite game, but it can still be a lot of fun. Pick someone to say, "No talking . . . starting NOW!" Then everyone has to be totally, completely quiet. No sniffing, no giggling, no noise at *all* or you're out of the game. You can set a short time limit, like five minutes, so you don't get bored.

Fun Facts: Being quiet is actually good for you. It lets your brain rest, improves your powers of creativity and observation, and sharpens your intelligence. Many people take temporary vows of silence to help draw attention to a cause, and some religious orders practice silence as a means of gaining a deeper understanding of their faith.

The Staring Game

WHO: anybody in the car who's not driving

WHAT YOU NEED: strong willpower

OBJECT: Try not to blink.

Siblings have been playing this game forever. If you're stuck in the backseat together, you might as well compete! Pick a partner, take a deep breath, and start staring. You *may not* blink—at all—and you *may not* break eye contact. If you do, your opponent wins. You can make faces or noises to try to break your partner's concentration, but beware: She'll probably try the same thing on you! If more than two people want to play, take turns. The winner of the first round plays the next contestant, the winner of that round plays whoever is next, and so on.

Fun Facts: This is a game, of course, but usually, staring at someone is considered rude or aggressive behavior. Staring directly into an animal's eyes can actually be dangerous, because they interpret it as a threat. So if you ever find yourself eye to eye with a big dog, a bear, or some other animal you don't know, start blinking, turn your head away, and let him win!!

Before You Play: Shuffling

Prior to any card game, you'll need to shuffle, or mix up, the cards. Remove the two joker cards and set them aside before you begin shuffling. Jokers aren't used in most games, but they're an essential part of others, so don't throw them away! Here are the two most common methods of shuffling:

Overhand Shuffle

This is the easiest shuffle. Pick up the deck of cards and hold it loosely in your nondominant hand. Slide a few cards forward, grasp them with your dominant hand, and place them on the bottom of the deck. Continue until you have worked your way through the entire deck. Simple as it seems, this is a very effective means of randomly mixing the cards.

Riffle Shuffle

In riffling, half of the deck is held in each hand. For each half deck, the thumb is placed over one short end, the ring and little fingers over the opposite short end, the knuckle of the middle finger in the center of the half deck, and the index finger over the top long edge. Hold the half decks very close together, with your thumbs touching and the cards only an inch or so above a table or other surface. While pressing down gently with your middle fingers, let your thumbs release the cards slowly so that they flutter down

to the table intertwined. (Your thumbs should move up the edge of the half deck as they let go of a few cards at a time.) When the entire deck is lying on the table, the half decks will be shuffled into each other about an inch or so; push the two together and neaten it back into a straight stack. It's likely that you will send the cards flying in all directions many times before you master this shuffle, but keep practicing and you'll eventually get it.

Cutting the Deck

If you're playing with strangers, you can offer to let them cut the deck, which gives them the opportunity to set aside the top portion of the deck and restack it to ensure that you have not arranged the cards for your benefit. If you're playing with people you know and trust, cutting the deck is not necessary. If you offer, your buddy might simply tap the top of the shuffled deck with his finger, which means, "It's fine. I trust you."

Now that your deck is all shuffled and ready to go, let's play some cards! Unless stated otherwise, the dealer usually deals to the left (clockwise) and deals himself the last card.

Aces Up

(also called Aces High, Drivel, Firing Squad, and Four Aces)

WHO: just you

WHAT YOU NEED: a deck of cards

OBJECT: Discard everything except the aces.

Lay down a row of four cards faceup. If any of the cards are the same suit, pick up the lower-value cards and stack them facedown to start a discard pile. Leave only the highest card of any suit. For example, if you lay down an 8 of diamonds, a jack of diamonds, a 2 of clubs, and a king of spades, you would discard the 8 of diamonds, leaving one empty space and three faceup cards. Aces have the highest value in this game, so if you have a king of hearts and an ace of hearts, you would discard the king.

When you can't discard any more cards, lay down four more faceup on top of the previous cards or in the empty spaces left by those you discarded. Layer new cards about a half inch down on top of any previous cards so that the value of the card underneath is visible. Again, if a suit shows up more than once, discard all but the highest-value card of that suit. Only cards at the tops of the piles can be played. If one of the four spots becomes empty, move a top card from any other pile into the empty space.

Repeat the process of laying down four new cards and discarding any lower-value cards of the same suit. The game is over when all the cards have been played. The goal is to discard all the cards except for the aces, leaving them the only cards upturned on the table.

Fun Facts: In some games, the ace is the card with the highest value. In other games, it is the card with the lowest value.

Beggar My Neighbor
(also called Beggar Your Neighbor and Beat Jack Out of Doors)

WHO: 2 or more players

WHAT YOU NEED: a deck of cards

OBJECT: To win all the cards.

Choose a dealer and have him deal out all the cards facedown in front of the players. The player to the left of the dealer starts the game by turning up his top card and playing it in the middle of the table. If the card has a value between 2 and 10, play passes to the left and the next player does the same thing. If a face card or an ace (called "court cards" in this game) is turned up, the next player must make a "payment" as follows:

> If an ace is played, the next player must turn over four cards, one at a time.
> If a king is played, the next player must turn over three cards, one at a time.
> If a queen is played, the next player must turn over two cards, one at a time.
> If a jack is played, the next player must turn over one card.

If all of the cards in the payment are number cards, the player who played the court card collects the whole stack of cards in the middle of the table. But if one of the payment cards is a court card, the player making the payment stops immediately, and the next player makes a payment to *him* based on the schedule above. If that player's payment contains only number cards, the cards in the middle of the table are collected by the last player who played a court card.

When a player wins the pile, she puts it at the bottom of her stack. Then the player to her left starts the next round by laying down his card in the center of the table. When a player runs out of cards, she's out of the game and the other players continue to play. The player who collects the entire deck of cards is the winner.

Tips

• This game can last a very long time, so unless it's a lazy day with nothing to do, you might want to set a time limit and decide that the player with the most cards at the end of that time is the winner.

Concentration
(also called Memory and Pairs)

WHO: 2 or more players

WHAT YOU NEED: a deck of cards

OBJECT: Get the most pairs.

Lay out all fifty-two cards facedown on the floor or table. Take turns turning over two cards at a time, trying to find a pair (two 5s, two jacks, etc.; the color and suit don't matter). If you get a match, pick up both cards, place them facedown in a pile beside you, and take another turn. If you don't turn over a match, your turn is over. The game ends when all the cards have been claimed. The winner is the player with the most pairs.

Tips

• When you don't get a match, try to remember which cards are where when you turn them back over. Later in the game, you may be able to remember that the card in the upper left corner was a queen, and so was the card over by your little brother's knee!

Variations

- Make this game harder by requiring that the two cards have to be of the same value *and* the same color.

- Make this game a little easier by arranging the cards in four rows of thirteen cards instead of just randomly placing them on the floor.

Crazy Eights

WHO: 2 or more players

WHAT YOU NEED: a deck of cards

OBJECT: Be the first player to get rid of all your cards.

Choose a dealer and have her deal out five cards to each player, then put the remaining cards facedown in the center of the table. This is the draw pile.

Players sort their hands by suit. The dealer turns over the top card of the draw pile to create a discard pile beside it. If the card she turns up is an 8—which, in this game, is a wild card and trumps (beats) all others, the dealer can choose any suit as the starting suit; otherwise, the starting suit is the same as the card she turned over.

Beginning with the player to the left of the dealer and moving clockwise, each player places a card from his hand faceup on the discard pile. It must be the same number, the same suit, or an 8. For example, if the top of the discard pile is the 6 of diamonds, you may play a 6 of any suit, a diamond of any value, or any of the four 8s. If it is a king of hearts, then you may play any king, heart, or 8. If you cannot match the number or suit and you do not have an 8, you must add cards from the draw pile to your hand, one by one, until you are able to make a play. (Once the draw pile is empty, players who cannot make a play must pass.) If you play an 8, you then pick what value or suit needs to be matched by the next player. When a player has only one card left in her hand, she must say "Last card!" The first person to get rid of all his cards is the winner.

- If only two people are playing, deal out seven cards instead of five.

- If you forget to say "Last card!" before the next person plays, you have to draw a card from the stockpile.

- If you have lots of players, you can use two decks to keep the game going longer.

Fifty-Two Card Pickup

WHO: 2 or more players

WHAT YOU NEED: a deck of cards

OBJECT: Trick someone into thinking this is a real game.

Ask someone if they'd like to play cards. If they say yes, pick up the deck of cards and act like you are about to shuffle them again. Then throw the cards up in the air so that they flutter back down on your unsuspecting victim. They get to play Fifty-Two Card Pickup now—as they pick up all fifty-two cards from wherever they have fallen!

Fun Facts: This is a favorite prank that experienced card players like to play on newbies.

Go Fish

WHO: 2–5 players

WHAT YOU NEED: a deck of cards

OBJECT: Get the most complete sets of card values.

. . . .

Choose a dealer and have her deal out seven cards to every player (or five, if there are lots of players). Put the remaining cards facedown on the table to be the stockpile.

The player to the left of the dealer begins the game by asking another player if he has any cards of a specific value, such as any 7s or any kings. (A player can only ask for a value that is a match to one she has in her hand.) If he does have any cards of that rank, the player must give all of them to the asker, who then requests another card from another player.

When someone doesn't have the card she requests, the one asked says "Go fish!" and the asker takes the top card from the stockpile. It then becomes the turn of the person to her left and play continues in the same way.

When a player collects all four cards of the same value (called a book), she places them facedown on the table next to her and continues playing. If a player runs out of cards, he is out of the game. The game ends when there are no cards left in the stockpile, and the player with the most books (sets of four) wins.

Fun Facts: Speaking of fish, did you know that a goldfish can live for more than *forty years*? Now there's a pet you can grow up with!

Hearts

WHO: 4 players

WHAT YOU NEED: a deck of cards, pencil and paper to keep score

OBJECT: Try not to get stuck with the queen of spades or any heart cards.

Choose a dealer and have her deal out all fifty-two cards; players can look at their hands. This game is played in four-card tricks, or rounds. For the first trick, the players select three cards from their hands and pass them facedown to the person on their left. Then whoever has the 2 of clubs goes first, or leads. That player lays down any card he likes, except a heart, in the center of the table. Starting with the player to the leader's left, all other players must play a card of the same suit (also called the trump suit) if they have one. If they do not have a card from that suit, they can lay down a card of any value from another suit (although they cannot win the trick with it). This is called sloughing, and is a great opportunity to get rid of cards you don't want or that might cause you problems later on.

GET RID OF THIS ONE ASAP!

Whoever lays down the highest card of the trump suit gets the trick and leads the next hand. The player claims the trick by collecting the four cards and turning them facedown on the table. (If a player gets subsequent tricks, he should arrange them crosswise or stacked separately so that he can see at a glance how many tricks he's taken.)

There are only two ways a player may lead a round with a heart: First, if she has nothing but hearts in her hand, she must lead with one. Otherwise, players must wait until hearts have been "broken," which means someone has sloughed a heart in a previous round. After that, players may lead with hearts whenever they choose.

Before the previous trick's winner lays down a card to start the second trick, all players pass three cards facedown to the player on their right, then the game resumes as before. At the beginning of the third round, all players pass three cards facedown to the player *across* from them, then the game resumes as before. No cards are passed at the beginning of the fourth round, but at the beginning of the fifth round, begin the four-round passing sequence again: three cards to the left, three cards to the right, three cards across the table, then a round with no cards passed.

Each heart counts as one point. The queen of spades counts as thirteen points. At the end of each trick, the points are tallied. The game ends when at least one player accumulates one hundred points. The person with the fewest points when that happens wins.

Fun Facts: And speaking of hearts: A healthy one pumps two thousand gallons of blood through your body's sixty thousand miles of blood vessels every day. Try to keep up with *that*, you vampires!

I Doubt It

(also called Cheat)

WHO: 3 or more players

WHAT YOU NEED: a deck of cards

OBJECT: Be the first player to get rid of all your cards.

Choose a dealer and have him deal out all fifty-two cards. If some players get more cards than others, that's okay. The player to the dealer's left begins the game by placing any aces he has in his hand facedown in the center of the table. This will become the discard pile. If the player doesn't have any aces, or if he wants to get rid of some of his cards, he can *pretend* to lay down aces by laying down whatever he wants (an ace and a 5, maybe, or three 8s) and saying "Two aces" or "Three aces," etc. This is called bluffing. (Don't get too carried away, though; no one's going to believe you have four aces in your hand!)

Moving clockwise, the play continues with the next player laying down any 2s in her hand. The player after that lays down 3s, then 4s, and so forth. Any time a player is suspicious of a declaration, she can call out, "I doubt it!" and the person who played the cards must turn them over and show the challenger whether he was bluffing or not. A player who is caught bluffing must pick up the *entire* discard pile and add it to his hand. If a challenged player is *not* bluffing, then the challenger has to pick up and add the discard pile to her hand.

If you make it all the way through from aces to kings and the game is still going, start again with aces. The first player to get rid of all his cards wins.

Tips

- Try to establish a reputation for honesty before you start bluffing. If you *always* bluff, no one's ever going to believe you!

- Don't tip people off to a bluff by laughing or your facial expressions. Have you ever heard the term "poker face"? That means your face gives no clue whatsoever as to what is—or isn't!—in your hand.

- If it's early in the game and you don't have much of a selection in your hand, accuse someone of bluffing when you're pretty sure they aren't. That way, you'll get to pick up the discard pile—all those cards might come in handy!

Odd One Out
(also called Old Maid)

WHO: 2 or more players

WHAT YOU NEED: a deck of cards

OBJECT: Try not to be the person left holding the unpaired queen (the old maid!).

Remove one queen (any suit) from the deck and set it aside. Choose a dealer and have him deal out the other fifty-one cards. All players set aside any pairs (two aces, two 7s, etc.) facedown on the table. Unpaired cards remain in players' hands.

The player to the dealer's left draws a card from the dealer's hand. If it makes a pair with a card in her own hand, she puts that pair facedown on the table. If it doesn't, she just keeps the card in her hand and her turn ends. The player to *that* person's left now draws a card from the previous player's hand, and the game continues in the same way. The game ends when one player is left holding a queen, thereby losing the game.

Pig

(also called Donkey, Hog, Spoons, and Tongues)

WHO: 3 or more

WHAT YOU NEED: a deck of cards (if you have more than thirteen players, you will need two decks of cards)

OBJECT: Get four of a kind, and don't be the P-I-G!

Go through the cards and select four cards, the same value of each suit, for each person playing. For example, if you have three players, you might select all the 7s, all the kings, and all the 10s. Set the rest of the deck aside and shuffle your selected cards.

Choose a dealer and have her deal four cards to each player. Everyone looks at their hands, chooses one card to discard, and passes it facedown to their left. The goal is to get four of a kind, so players get rid of anything that won't help them do that. They then pick up the card coming to them from their right (another player's discard), add it to their hand, and choose a new card to pass to the left. No one should ever have more than four cards in his hand at any time.

Play continues in this way until someone gets four of a kind. Passing can happen as slowly or as quickly as you wish. As soon as you have four of something in your hand (four 4s, four heart cards, four jacks, etc.), quickly and quietly place your finger on your nose. If you don't have four of a kind but you see a player put a finger on *his* nose, hurry up and do the same—because the last player to put a finger on her nose gets a letter: first a *P*, then an *I*, then a *G*. The first person to get all three letters and be a PIG loses the game.

Variations

- Play D-O-N-K-E-Y instead of P-I-G, which will make the game last longer.

- Deal out the whole deck instead of just four cards per person (although everyone should still have an equal number of cards in their hands). This makes the game much longer.

- To play Spoons, lay out several spoons in the center of the table. There should be one less spoon than there are players. When you get four of a kind, instead of putting your finger on your nose, take a spoon. When other players see you take a spoon, they should take one, too. Whoever is last to notice will get a *P* instead of a spoon!

- To play Tongues, instead of putting your finger on your nose when you get four of a kind, stick out your tongue. Last player to stick out his tongue gets a *P*.

Fun Facts: Pigs play in the mud because they don't have sweat glands and that's how they cool themselves off. What's *your* excuse?

Rummy

WHO: 2 to 6 players

WHAT YOU NEED: a deck of cards

OBJECT: Be the first player to get rid of all your cards.

Choose a dealer and have him deal out the cards. If only two people are playing, each player gets ten cards. If there are three or four players, deal out seven cards each, and if there are five or six players, each one gets six cards each. Place the remaining cards facedown in the center of the table to serve as the stockpile. Take

the top card from the stockpile and place it faceup next to the stockpile. This will be the discard pile.

The goal in Rummy is to form "melds" (a set of three or four of a certain value, such as the 6 of hearts, 6 of spades, and 6 of diamonds) or "runs" (three or more cards in numerical or rank order of the same suit, such as the 9, 10, and jack of clubs). Each player looks at his hand and arranges it to make it easy to keep track of melds and runs. The player on the dealer's left begins the game by choosing the top card from either the stockpile or the discard pile. If you can make any melds or runs, lay them down faceup in front of you so that the number value of all cards is visible. If you have at least one card left in your hand, place one on the discard pile faceup. If you laid down all your cards in melds or runs (it does happen!), you can declare "Rummy." You can only declare "Rummy" if you have not previously laid down a meld or a run.

The next player draws a card from either the stockpile or the discard pile, then lays down any melds or runs she has. If she has at least one run or meld, she may also lay down cards that match the first player's melds or runs. For example, if the first player laid down three 7s and a diamond run of 3, 4, and 5, the second player could lay down a fourth 7, a 2 of diamonds, or a 6 and 7 of diamonds. (Put your matches in front of you, not on your neighbors' cards, or you may forget to count those points at the end of the game.) When she is through laying down cards, the player sets one card on the discard pile.

If the stockpile runs out of cards, set aside the top card of the discard pile and turn the rest of it facedown to become the new stockpile. Play continues until a player gets rid of all his cards.

Tally points as follows: Aces are worth one point, face cards are worth ten points, and number cards are worth that number. (A 7 of spades is worth seven points.) Count up the points of all the cards you laid on the table, then deduct points for every card still in your hand. That is your final score. The first player to five hundred (or whatever number you set) is the winner.

Fun Facts: Rummy has always been one of America's most popular card games. It was a favorite pastime in saloons during California's Gold Rush days and in Hollywood movie studios during the 1940s.

Sevens

(also called Card Dominoes, Fan Tan, and Parliament)

WHO: 2 or more players

WHAT YOU NEED: a deck of cards

OBJECT: Be the first player to get rid of all your cards.

Choose a dealer and have her deal out all fifty-two cards. The players pick up and sort their cards by suit. The player who holds the 7 of diamonds starts the game by placing this card faceup in the center of the table. The next player (to the left of the first player) lays down a card of the same suit either numerically above or below the 7 (in this case, either the 6 or 8 of diamonds). This card should be placed on either side of the 7 card, the 8 on one side and the 6 on the other. If the player has neither of those cards, but does have a 7 in a different suit, she lays down her 7 below the 7 of diamonds, and her turn is over. If the player has neither a 6 or 8 of diamonds nor a 7 of another suit, she must pass.

If the 6 or 8 of diamonds was just played, the next player can play a 5 on the 6, or a 9 on the 8. These cards are laid on top of the card being built upon. He can also play a 7 of another suit, placing it above or below the existing 7s. If he has none of these cards, then he must pass.

If a new 7 was just played, the next player then has the original choice of playing a 6 or 8 of diamonds, plus the new choice of playing a 6 or 8 of whatever suit the new 7 is. If he has none of those cards and no 7 of another suit to start another row, then he must pass.

Players continue the numerical sequences on the various stacks, building up or down from the cards on the table. The first player to use up all her cards is the winner.

Slapjack

WHO: 2 to 6 players

WHAT YOU NEED: a deck of cards

OBJECT: Try to get all the cards.

. . . .

Choose a dealer and have him deal out all fifty-two cards. Each player puts his cards in a pile facedown in front of him, without looking at them. The player to the dealer's left chooses the top card from his pile and places it faceup in the center of the table. If it's a jack, everyone tries to be the first person to slap the card. Whoever hits the jack first gets to claim the card and put it on the bottom of his card pile. If the card played *isn't* a jack, players continue placing cards on the pile one by one. When the next jack appears, whoever slaps it gets to claim *all* the cards under it.

If you accidentally slap a card that is *not* a jack, you have to give the top card from your own pile to the player whose card you accidentally slapped. If you run out of cards, you can stay in the game and try extra hard to slap the next jack that shows up to replenish your hand. The game ends when one person has all the cards.

Fun Facts: Jack is an extremely popular name in the United Kingdom and Australia, although not *so* much in America. Still, there are an awful lot of famous Jacks in the world; just in nursery rhymes *alone*, there's Jack Sprat who ate no fat, Jack who climbed the beanstalk, Jack who went up the hill with Jill, Jack who jumped over the candlestick, and Jack who stuck his finger in a pie. No *wonder* Jacks are always getting slapped!

Snap

WHO: 2 or more players

WHAT YOU NEED: a deck of cards (including the jokers)

OBJECT: Try to get all the cards.

Choose a dealer and have him deal out all fifty-two cards. Players gather their cards into stacks and place them, facedown, on the table in front of them. Then players count together, "One, two, three." On the word *three*, players turn over the top card of their pile. If any of the card values match (for example, two jacks or three 3s; suits don't matter in this game), the first player to yell "Snap!" gets the cards. If multiple players yell "Snap!" at the same time, no one gets the cards. If no two flipped cards have the same value, then players repeat, "One, two, three," and flip over another round of cards. Cards are flipped over into piles until matching cards appear, and whoever says "Snap!" first then wins the whole pile. If you yell "Snap!" accidentally and the cards don't match, you have to give your opponent one of your own cards. Jokers are wild cards and can be a match for anything. Whoever ends up with all the cards is the winner.

Variations

• Turn it into Animal Snap. Each person decides what animal they will be. Play exactly as above, except when you spot a match, instead of yelling "Snap!" you make the sound of the matching card owners' animals. For example, if the player next to you is a wolf and the player across from you is a turkey, and you see that their cards match, if you're the first person to howl and gobble, you get to claim all the turned over cards in those players' piles.

Snip Snap Snorum

(also called the Earl of Coventry)

WHO: 3 or more players

WHAT YOU NEED: a deck of cards

OBJECT: Be the first player to get rid of all your cards.

Choose a dealer and have him deal out all the cards. Players sort their hands by value (suit doesn't matter in this game). The player on the dealer's left chooses a card and lays it, faceup, in the center of the table. Moving clockwise, the next player lays down a card of the same value (remember, suit doesn't matter) and yells "Snip!" If she doesn't have a card that matches, she must pass. Play continues in the same way, with the next person who lays down a match yelling "Snap!" and the person after that (who is holding the fourth matching card) yelling "Snorum!" The player who yelled "Snorum!" then gets to lay down a new card and play continues. The first player to get rid of all his cards is the winner.

Solitaire

(also called Idiot's Delight, Klondike, and Patience)

WHO: just you

WHAT YOU NEED: a deck of cards

OBJECT: Divide all four suits into complete, rank-ordered stacks.

Lay down seven cards horizontally, facedown, on the table in front of you. Turn the first card on the left faceup; leave the others facedown. Skipping the first card that is faceup, repeat the process. (You'll only use six cards this time.) Turn over the top card in the second stack, and leave the others facedown. Repeat this process, laying down cards on fewer and fewer stacks each time, until you lay down only one card on the very last stack (the seventh one) and turn it back over immediately. You should have used up twenty-eight cards to create this tableau, as it's called. Set aside the rest of the cards, facedown, to be your stockpile.

If the top card on any of your seven stacks is an ace, remove it from its stack and place it, faceup, above the existing row of cards. This row of four aces is called your foundation. Any time an ace shows up on one of your seven stacks or the stockpile, move it up to the foundation. As soon as you reposition an ace from one of the seven stacks, turn over the top card of that stack.

In the foundation, sequences are built by ascending number and suit. Once you have an ace in your foundation, you can build on top of it with the 2 of the same suit, then the 3, and so on. When you lay down a card on one of the four foundations, stack it directly on top of the previous card.

If there are no aces in your top cards, start building on the cards by stacking them in descending value. For instance, if you have a king of diamonds in your second row and a queen of spades in another row, move the queen on top of the king. There is a slight catch, though: The cards have to be not only in numeric order, but also in alternating colors. For example, if the top card on the first stack is a 9 of hearts (red), and you turn over an 8 of clubs (black) on the fourth stack, immediately place that card on top of the 9 of hearts. *Remember: sequential numbers, but alternating colors in the tableau.* When you lay down a card on top of another in the tableau, leave about a half inch of the previous card showing, so that you can see the numbers/colors cascading down. Once you have moved a card onto another stack, remember to flip over the facedown card that is now showing on that pile.

Any time you cannot play any of the top cards in your tableau, draw a card from the stockpile. If there is no place to play a card you draw or turn over, lay it facedown beside you as a waste pile.

Whenever you can move an entire cascade, or sequence, on top of another, do so. For example, if the fifth stack has a 10 of diamonds, a 9 of clubs, and an 8 of hearts, and the second stack has a 7 of spades and a 6 of hearts, pick up that 7 of spades and 6 of hearts and add them to the fifth stack sequence. Then go back and turn over the top card of the second stack and see where it can be played, or what could be played on top of *it*.

At some point, you will deplete one or more of your seven stacks. When a stack is depleted, you can fill that empty space with any king you turn over or that is currently showing. For example, if moving that 7 of spades and 6 of hearts from the second stack left that space empty instead of leaving more cards to turn over, and there's a king of hearts, a queen of clubs, a jack of diamonds, and a 10 of clubs cascading down on the seventh stack, pick up all the turned-up cards, from the king through the 10 of clubs, and move them, in order, to the open space where the second stack used to be. That way you can reveal the cards previously hidden beneath the king of hearts. Be careful when you lift and move cards so that they remain in the same order.

Play continues with you turning over, shifting, or drawing cards until you have separated the cards into four piles of sequential suits, with the ace on the bottom and the king on top. Any time you run out of cards in your stockpile, shuffle the waste pile, turn it facedown, and it becomes your new stockpile.

Fun Facts: There are more than a thousand variations of solitaire, so if someone says, "Hey, that's not the way you play," she may just have learned a different version. Teach each other your respective variations, and that's one more cool game you'll know how to play!

Spades

WHO: 4 players

WHAT YOU NEED: a deck of cards, pencil and paper to keep score

OBJECT: Be the first team to get 500 points.

HOW TO PLAY:

Divide players into two teams. Sit so that partners face each other across the table. Choose someone to deal first. (Each player will take a turn at dealing.) Have him deal out all fifty-two cards, beginning with the player to his left and with the dealer receiving the last card. Players study their hands to determine how many sets of four cards, or tricks, they think they can win. There are thirteen rounds in a set.

Spades are trump in this game, meaning they overrule all other suits, so if you have a lot of spades in your hand, particularly high ones, you should bid higher. Having the ace or king usually guarantees a trick. Having no cards of a suit at all (for example, having no hearts), or no more than one, is also usually good for a trick because you can use a spade to trump whenever someone

leads that suit. If you don't think you'll win any tricks (if you have no face cards, only one or two low spades, and a fairly even mix of the other suits), you should probably bid one instead of none (called nil or null), because if you unexpectedly win a trick when you've declared you will take none, it will cost you ten points. However, a successful null bid will win you one hundred points. You and your partner will combine your bids, so don't get carried away. If you think you can take seven tricks and your partner thinks she can take six, that means you have absolutely *no* margin for error. You want to bid accurately (because you get ten points for every trick you predicted you would get, but only one point for those you didn't count on), but don't be overconfident until you get some experience. If your opponent has no diamonds at *all* in her hand, that ace of diamonds you counted as a sure thing may be dead in the water!

Choose someone to keep score. That person makes two columns on a piece of paper—one for each team, with the players' names at the top. As you reveal your bids, beginning with the player on the dealer's left, the scorekeeper writes them down on either side of the column, with the partners' combined numbers written in the middle. For example:

<u>James/Jaron</u>   <u>John/Jose</u>

   2   5   3   1   8   7

Play begins with the player to the dealer's left laying down a card. Spades have to be "broken," or turned to of necessity, before they can be used, so if you have the ace of spades you can't lead with that. All other aces, however, make great lead cards because they will almost always guarantee a trick—early in the game, especially. Do not, under *any* circumstance, lead with a king unless you are also holding the ace. If you have no really high cards, play it safe with something middle-of-the-road, such as a 7 or 8. This is high enough to lure out your opponents' higher cards, but low enough to let your partner take the lead if he can.

After the first player has put down a card, the other players follow suit—literally. Your card must be the same suit as the first card that was laid down. If you do not have a card of the same suit, you may play a different one, although you cannot win the trick with it, or you may play a spade. Spade carefully; *you* may not have any clubs, but your partner might have a handful. Don't make her waste a queen unless it's unavoidable. Things can get quite interesting when one partner discovers the other is out of cards in a suit, or void; he can then keep laying down that suit in the hope that his partner has a ready supply of spades to keep trumping.

Whoever lays down the highest card in a round gets to take the trick and leads the next round. (One partner usually collects the tricks for each team, stacking them neatly on top of one another in a staggered cascade, out of the way of play.) Remember that spades are trumps, so if you laid down a jack on top of a 2 and a 7 but somebody trumped it with a 2 of spades, that player gets the trick instead of you.

Once all thirteen rounds have been played, players count their tricks and figure out their scores. If you got what you bid, you simply add a zero to your score, like this:

James/Jaron

2 50 3

John/Jose

1 80 7

If you got fewer tricks than you bid, you lose ten points for each point you originally bid (even though you won some of them). For example, if your team bid five but only got three, you lose fifty points for that round.

You/Your Partner

2 -50 3

If you got the tricks you predicted plus a couple you didn't, you only get one point each for those extra tricks. For example, if you bid five but won seven, you score fifty-two.

You/Your Partner

2 52 3

Anyone who goes null gets a hundred points, in addition to whatever her partner bid. (Be careful with null bids; it's easy to *lose* a hundred points instead of gaining them!) For example, let's say you went null and your partner bid three. At the end of the round, you took no tricks (as expected, with that lousy hand of yours!), but your partner took five tricks instead of the three he expected. (This would be natural, since he would have been trying to help you not to get any tricks and would likely have gotten at least one extra.) Your score will be 132—one hundred for your successful null bid, thirty for his successful three bid, plus two points for the tricks he didn't anticipate. This is what it would look like on paper:

You/Your Partner

0 132 3

Once everyone's score is figured out and recorded, the player to the left of the last dealer gathers, shuffles, and deals the cards as before, and play continues. The first team to get five hundred points is the winner.

Tips

- If things are getting desperate, you can go "blind null." Your team must be at least two hundred points behind and you must declare your blind null bid before the dealer deals. After all the cards are dealt, choose your two most threatening cards (definitely any high spades, or maybe face cards if you only have one or two cards in that suit) and pass those to your partner. At the same time, he passes you his two least threatening cards (something like a 2 or 3 of any suit except spades). Play then continues as normal. If you get through the round without taking any tricks, you earn two hundred points, plus whatever your partner bid. If that 3 of hearts (or that queen of spades you got stuck with after you passed the ace and the king to your partner!) manages to be the high card somewhere along the way, though, you have just lost two hundred points and are in worse shape than ever.

Speed
(also called Spit)

WHO: 2 players

WHAT YOU NEED: a deck of cards

OBJECT: Be the first player to get rid of your cards.

Deal out all the cards so that each player has half the deck. Arrange them, starting on each player's left, in five stacks as follows: a stack of five cards with the top card turned over; next to that, a stack of four, then a stack of three, two, and one (the top cards turned over on all stacks). These are called your stockpiles. Players place the rest of their cards in the middle of the table, forming two piles of spit cards.

Both players call out, "One, two, three, spit!" and each player, using only one hand, turns over their top spit card, placing it beside the stack. This will form your spit pile.

From this point on, the goal is to play the cards in your stockpiles onto either of the two spit piles before your opponent can do the same. A card can only be played if it is in numerical order (either increasing or decreasing) of the faceup cards on either of the two spit piles. For example, if the middle piles show a jack and a 3, you could lay down a 10 or a queen on the jack, or a 2 or a 4 on the 3. Suits and colors don't matter in this game, only value, and aces can be played either after a king or before a 2.

As soon as you play a card from one of your stockpile stacks, flip over the one underneath it. You can never have more than five stockpiles, but if you use up one of the piles, you can take a faceup card off another pile and start a new one in the empty space.

If the game reaches a point where neither player can play any cards from their stockpiles, take a breath, then both say, "One, two, three, spit!" again and turn over the top card of the spit pile to get things moving again. This procedure can be repeated as often as necessary. The game ends when someone runs out of cards.

War

WHO: 2 players

WHAT YOU NEED: a deck of cards

OBJECT: Get all your opponent's cards.

Deal out all the cards, facedown, then players gather them in their hands in a neat stack without looking at them. Both players flip out the top card in their stack, at the same time, and lay it faceup in the center of the table, side by side. Whoever turns over the higher-ranking card gets to collect both cards and put them on the bottom of her stack. (The ace is the high card in this game.) Repeat this process until two cards of the same value (two 6s, for example) show up, then it's War!

When players turn up cards of the same value, each player takes four cards from her stack, puts three facedown on top of the card that is facing up in the middle of the table, then tops it with the fourth card, facing up. Whoever has the higher ranking faceup card this time wins all the cards in the middle of the table. If the two cards turned faceup are again of the same value, it's War again: Turn another three cards facedown on top of the pile and then another faceup. This can be repeated as many times as matching cards appear.

Play continues in this way, with War taking place anytime two cards of equal value appear. Whoever gets all the cards is the winner.

Variations

- Three people can play this game if you remove one card from the deck and set it aside so everyone has seventeen cards. If two of the three cards turned up are of equal value, all three players go to War.

Blindman's Buff

(also called Blindman's Bluff and Blindman)

WHO: 3 or more players

WHAT YOU NEED: a large room or outdoor area with no obstacles

OBJECT: Try to find another player while blindfolded.

Choose someone to be It. Put a blindfold on him and spin him in place five times while everyone else finds a hiding spot. When he stops spinning, It yells, "Stop!" and everyone must freeze and stop moving, wherever they are. It tries to find players while still blindfolded. Players are not allowed to move their feet, but can dodge or bend to try to keep It from touching them. Once It tags a player, that person gets to be It.

Variations

• Instead of freezing in place, players can move around and make all kinds of weird noises to confuse or distract It.

• When It catches someone, she feels that person's face and tries to guess who it is. If she's right, that person becomes It. If she's wrong, It must try to find another player.

• When It catches someone, that person is out of the game. Play continues until It has tagged everyone.

• If you play this game in a swimming pool, it's called Marco Polo.

Fun Facts: Blindman's Buff was invented more than two thousand years ago. It was especially popular in England during the reign of King Henry VIII.

Bobbing for Apples

WHO: 2 or more players

WHAT YOU NEED: a clean, wide, deep tub filled with fresh water and whole apples; towels to put around the base of the tub (if you're playing indoors) and to dry off players; a table to put the tub on, if you don't want it on the floor

OBJECT: Be the first player to bite and retrieve an apple from the tub.

Figure out how many people can fit around the tub at one time, then have that many players circle around the tub with their arms behind their backs. Have someone yell "Go!" The first player to bite and hold on to an apple and stand back from the tub is the winner. If you have a large group, the winners from each small group can compete against one another to determine the overall winner. If the tub is too small for multiple bobbers, you can time each player as they bob individually, and the quickest player wins.

Tips

- Remove all stems and leaves from apples.

- Keep the water level at least five or six inches below the top of the tub so it doesn't slosh over when things get lively.

- Big, crisp apples are harder to catch than small, soft ones.

Variations

- If the tub is up high, players can stand around it and bend over. If the tub is on the floor, players can be on their knees and bend over.

- Designate one particular apple as a prize apple that comes with a special reward.

- Instead of putting apples in a tub of water, stretch a cord across an area (between two trees, for instance, or from one side of a room to the other), tie apples by their stems to the cord, and let players try to bite and hold on to one.

Button, Button, Who's Got the Button?

WHO: 6 or more players

WHAT YOU NEED: a large button

OBJECT: Guess who has the button.

Decide who is It. It holds her hands together, with the button between her palms and with her thumbs on top. Other players sit or stand in a circle around It with their hands in front of them, palms together, their thumbs on top. It goes around the circle, placing her hands on top of everyone else's, pretending to put the button in their hands. She actually *does* deposit the button in one person's hands, but continues to go all the way around the circle so no one knows where the button is. When It has gone all the way around the circle, she goes to stand in the middle of the circle and asks, "Button, button, who's got the button?" Then she goes around the circle again, with each player guessing who has the button. If the person who *has* the button hasn't yet been identified when it's his turn, he pretends to guess someone else's name. When the player with the button is finally identified, he gets to be It.

Variations

• It stands in the center of the circle. Players pass the button around behind their backs. At some point, somebody keeps the button, but pretends to pass it on, as do all of the other players after that point. It has to guess who has the button. If he does so correctly, he takes the place of that player in the circle, and the player who had the button becomes It.

Fun Facts: Have you ever noticed the buttons on the sleeves of men's suit coats? They really don't serve any purpose; they're just *there*. Rumor has it that it's a leftover tradition from the eighteenth century, when King Frederick the Great ordered buttons to be sewn on his soldiers' sleeves so they wouldn't use them to wipe their noses!

Capture the Flag

WHO: 10 or more players, evenly divided into 2 teams

WHAT YOU NEED: a large open area, 2 "flags" (bandannas, hand towels, scarves, or similar small pieces of cloth), a piece of rope or hose to serve as a dividing line

OBJECT: Capture the other team's flag and get home safely.

Divide a large area equally, using a hose or rope to mark the dividing line. Each team determines a home base and a jail for themselves, and also chooses a place from which to fly their team's flag. The flag should be very visible. The object of this game is to find and capture the flag of the opposing team and carry it back into your team's territory without being tagged. If a player gets tagged while in enemy territory, he becomes a prisoner and must go to jail. If he has the flag when he's tagged, the flag goes back to where it came from. A teammate can free prisoners by sneaking in and tagging them, but both rescuer and prisoners must go all the way back to their own territory before attempting to capture the flag again. The team that captures their opponents' flag and safely returns to their own territory with it wins.

Tips

- Dressing teams in different colors or having some other identifying mark (baseball caps, armbands) will make it easier to keep up with who's who.

- Always leave at least one team member guarding the flag.

- Try to distract your opponents with random outbursts or organized plans of attack.

Variations

- Only one prisoner can be freed at a time.

- Prisoners can hold hands and make a chain to help them get closer to a free team member so she can tag them.

Fun Facts: Capture the Flag has been played since the Middle Ages.

Cat and Mouse

WHO: 6 or more players

WHAT YOU NEED: lots of energy

OBJECT: Keep the Cat away from the Mouse.

Choose one player to be the Mouse and one player to be the Cat. Everyone else holds hands in a circle and walks or dances around together. The Cat stands outside the circle; the Mouse stands inside the circle. The Mouse says, "I'm the mouse, you can't catch me!" Then the Cat says, "I'm the cat; we'll see! We'll see!" The Cat then tries to catch the Mouse. Players raise their hands up and down at random, trying to protect the Mouse; the Mouse and the Cat can only come in and out of the circle if hands are up. If the Mouse gets caught, he takes a place in the circle, the Cat becomes the new Mouse, and a new player is chosen to be the Cat.

Variations

- Make this game more fun by having the Cat mew pitifully if he gets caught inside the circle, trying to convince someone to let him out. If that doesn't work, he can get feisty and try to break through someone's hands with a mean old "MEOW!"

- Instead of forming a circle, players can line up in three or four rows, holding hands to create a sort of maze or obstacle course. Choose a director, then everyone yells, "Ready, steady, go!" and the Cat chases the Mouse through the rows. Periodically, the director can complicate things by yelling, "Change! Turn right!" or

"Change! Turn left!" and everyone drops hands and follows the directions, grabbing the hands of their new neighbors and creating different rows.

- Instead of a cat and a mouse, you can make your animals a fox and a rabbit, a lion and a gazelle, or some other pairing.

- Turn this into Shark and Swimmer by playing in the shallow end of a swimming pool.

Colored Eggs

WHO: 4 or more players

WHAT YOU NEED: a large area with no obstacles, a designated goal such as a tree or fence line

OBJECT: Don't get caught by the wolf.

Choose someone to be the wolf; everyone else is an egg. The eggs line up next to one another, and each thinks of a color. (Basic is best; it's not likely the wolf is going to think of cornflower blue or magenta.) The wolf shouts, "Knock, knock!" and everyone says, "Who's there?" Then the wolf replies, "A big smelly wolf with snow white hair—and I want some eggs!" and everyone says, "What color?" When the wolf names a color, everyone who picked that color tries to run to the goal and back without getting caught by the wolf. If the wolf catches a player before he makes it back to his place in line, that player becomes the wolf and the current wolf takes that player's place in line.

Fun Facts: Getting enough to eat is a full-time job for wolves, so they'd love this game! Eggs (colored or not!) aren't wolves' favorite food, though; they prefer large, hoofed animals such as deer, elk, or mountain goats, or medium-sized ones like rabbits or beavers. When pickings are slim, though, they'll eat anything from grasshoppers to blackberries.

Crab Race

WHO: any number of players

WHAT YOU NEED: flexibility and speed

OBJECT: Be the first crab to the finish line.

Determine a starting line and a finish line. Sit on the ground with your hands behind you and your knees bent in front of you so that your feet, bottom, and hands are on the ground. Now lift your bottom and "crab-walk" your way to the finish line. You can walk backward, forward, or sideways—whichever method will get you to the finish line first!

Variations

- If you have at least six or eight players, make this game more fun by making it a relay race. Form two equal teams, have someone shout "Go!" and let the first player from each team take off. They need to crab-walk to the finish line, then crab-walk back and tag the next player, who repeats that procedure. The first team to get all its players to the finish line and back is the winner.

Fun Facts: Crabs are *not* very nice. They're greedy and aggressive and always looking to pick a fight. But if *you* had to walk like that all the time, you might be cranky, too!

Doggie, Doggie

WHO: 6 or more players

WHAT YOU NEED: a "bone" (can be a small stone or block, a chalkboard eraser, or even an actual dog bone or biscuit)

OBJECT: Guess correctly who took your bone.

Pick someone to be the doggie. He sits at the front of the room, facing away from everyone else with his eyes closed. Place the "bone" under the doggie's chair. Everyone else sits in a semicircle behind the doggie. One player sneaks up, takes the bone, and returns to her seat, hiding the bone so it can't be seen. Then everyone says:

> Doggie, doggie, who's got the bone?
> Someone stole it from your home.
> Guess who, maybe you,
> Maybe the monkey from the zoo.
> Wake up, doggie. Find your bone!

The doggie then opens his eyes, turns around, and gets three guesses as to who took his bone. If he guesses correctly, he takes that player's spot in the circle and that player becomes the doggie. If, after three guesses, he still hasn't identified the thief, his turn is over and someone else gets to be the doggie.

Variations

- Don't make the doggie stop after three guesses; let him guess until he correctly identifies the thief. That person then becomes the new doggie.

- Choose a doggie and one other player and have everyone else form a circle, sitting on the ground with their hands behind their backs. The doggie stands in the middle of the circle and covers her eyes. The other player holds the bone in his hands and walks slowly around the outside of the circle while everyone says the rhyme. At some point she discreetly drops the bone into the hands of another player, then takes a seat with the others. When the rhyme ends, the doggie opens her eyes and gets three chances to guess who has the bone. If she guesses correctly, she takes that player's spot in the circle and that player becomes the doggie. If she doesn't guess, the person who hid the bone becomes the doggie.

Drop the Handkerchief

(also called I Wrote a Letter to My Mother and Rag Tag)

WHO: 6 or more players

WHAT YOU NEED: a handkerchief or bandanna

OBJECT: Catch the person who dropped the handkerchief.

Choose someone to be It. Everyone else sits in a circle facing inward. It walks around the outside of the circle carrying a handkerchief, then randomly drops it behind a player. As soon as that player realizes the handkerchief is behind him, he gets up, grabs it, and chases after It, trying to tag her. It tries to get around the circle and back to that player's empty spot before getting tagged. If she makes it to the empty spot, the player chasing her becomes It and the game begins again. If It gets caught, however, she must go into the middle of the circle and can't come out until someone else comes in; the other player becomes It.

Variations

• Change this game by using an envelope or a piece of junk mail instead of a handkerchief and have everyone sing this song as It walks around the outside of the circle:

> A tisket, a tasket,
> a green and yellow basket.
> Wrote a letter to my mother,
> on the way I dropped it.
> I dropped it, I dropped it,
> on the way I dropped it.
> One of you has picked it up
> and put it in your pocket.

Then It says, as he passes each player, "Not you, not you, not you . . ." until he suddenly declares, ". . . but YOU!" and drops the letter behind a player. The game continues as above.

Fun Facts: Drop the Handkerchief has been played for centuries. It was especially popular during the colonial days of America.

Duck, Duck, Goose

WHO: 8 or more players

WHAT YOU NEED: room to run

OBJECT: Tag It before he gets back to the free space.

. . . .

Choose someone to be It. Everyone else sits in a circle, facing inward. It walks around the circle and taps each player on the head (gently!), saying "duck" each time, until he suddenly proclaims one player a "goose" instead. (There is no set number of players that must be ducks. It might tap two ducks, or ten ducks, before choosing a goose.) The goose jumps up and chases It, trying to catch him before he gets back to sit in the goose's empty spot. If It succeeds in getting away, the goose becomes It and the game begins again. If the goose tags It, however, the goose goes back to his seat and It begins the "duck, duck, goose" routine again.

Variations

. . . .

• When the goose is picked, It runs in one direction around the circle while the goose runs the other direction. Whoever gets to the goose's empty spot first sits down, and the other player is It.

• If the goose tags It, It has to sit in the center of the circle (the "stew pot" or "mush pot") and the goose becomes It. When there are more people in the stew pot than in the circle, you can end the game or start again. Or you can let the person in the middle out when a new It is tagged and enters the stew pot.

• If you're at the beach or pool, turn this into Duck, Duck, Splash: It walks around the circle with a pail of water, tapping and pronouncing every player a duck until she randomly says "Splash!" and pour the water over that player's head. The player who got splashed jumps up and tries to tag It, just like in the regular game.

Egg Toss

WHO: 5 or more players

WHAT YOU NEED: a raw egg for every pair of players

OBJECT: Toss your egg back and forth without breaking it.

Choose a leader, then have everyone else choose a partner. Line up all partners, facing each other, in two straight lines, about two feet apart. Give a raw egg to all the players on one side. When the leader yells "Toss!" the players holding the eggs toss them to their partners. Anyone who drops an egg or whose egg breaks is immediately out of the game. Everyone else takes one step back, and when the leader yells "Toss!" they toss their egg back to their partners. Anyone who drops an egg or whose egg breaks is out of the game, and the game continues as before. The last team with an intact egg wins.

Tips

• If you're catching the egg, hold your hands up to meet it, then quickly lower them as the egg begins to settle into your hands. It will keep the egg from crash-landing and give it a little extra cushion.

Variations

• If it's hot as blazes outside, turn this into a *very* cool game by replacing the eggs with water balloons!

Fun Facts: Egg tossing (or egg throwing, as it's called in England) dates back to the 1300s. Legend says that the Abbot of Swaton, in Lincolnshire, offered parishioners an egg in exchange for attendance at church services. When the river flooded, preventing the peasants from getting to church, monks hurled the eggs across to them. True? No one knows—but there *is* a World Egg Throwing Federation . . . and it's based in Swaton.

Feather

WHO: 3 or more players

WHAT YOU NEED: a small, fluffy feather

OBJECT: Keep the feather in the air and don't let it touch you.

. . . .

Players sit in a circle. One player throws the feather as high into the air as possible, then everyone takes turns blowing the feather to keep it in the air and not let it touch them. If the feather touches a player, she is out of the game. The last person remaining in the game is the winner.

Fun Facts: Feather was a favorite at British parties during the time of Queen Victoria's reign.

Follow the Leader

WHO: 3 or more players

WHAT YOU NEED: good eyes

OBJECT: Do what the leader does.

. . . .

Choose someone to be the leader. Everyone lines up behind her, single file. The leader walks around the room making crazy motions or doing funny movements; everyone else must follow her lead and do exactly the same thing. For example, if the leader puts her fingers on her head like antennae, everyone else must do that, too. If the leader starts cawing like a crow, everyone else must do that, too. Anyone who doesn't is out of the game. The last person in the game (besides the leader) is the winner.

Fun Facts: Being a good leader takes some special skills. You need to be confident, creative, enthusiastic, clear in your instructions, and consistent in your message. The better you are at leading, the easier it is for people to follow you—whether it's in this game or in something else, like a project at school.

Ghost in the Graveyard

WHO: 3 or more players

WHAT YOU NEED: room to run with 2 designated bases, such as trees, big rocks, buildings, etc., at either end of the area

OBJECT: Don't get turned into a ghost!

Choose someone to be the ghost. Everyone else gathers at the base at one end of the play area, closes their eyes, and says:

> One o'clock, the ghost's not here,
> Two o'clock, the ghost's not here,
> Three o'clock, the ghost's not here,
> Four o'clock, the ghost's not here,
> Five o'clock, the ghost's not here,
> Six o'clock, the ghost's not here,
> Seven o'clock, the ghost's not here,
> Eight o'clock, the ghost's not here,
> Nine o'clock, the ghost's not here,
> Ten o'clock, the ghost's not here,
> Eleven o'clock, he's getting near,
> Midnight! Ghost appear!

While everyone else is reciting the rhyme, the ghost hides somewhere between the two bases. At the end of the rhyme, players open their eyes and make their way toward the other base, searching along the way for the ghost. The ghost can hide as long as she likes. Once a player spots her, he must yell, "Ghost in the graveyard!" and everyone runs to the other base as quickly as possible while the ghost chases them. Anybody the ghost tags becomes a ghost, and the game continues until only one player is left who is not a ghost. That person is the winner. .

Variations

- Players can just count to fifty or one hundred instead of reciting the rhyme.

- Make this game a little spooky and a lot of fun by playing at night. Give every player a flashlight and make sure there's nothing to trip over in your playing area.

Heads Up, Seven Up

(also called Heads Up, Thumbs Up)

WHO: 14 or more players

WHAT YOU NEED: your deductive reasoning

OBJECT: Identify the person who pushes down your thumb.

Choose a leader, then choose seven players to stand at the front of the play area. Everyone else spreads out and sits down. The leader says, "Heads down, thumbs up!" and all but the chosen seven close their eyes, bow their heads, and hold up a fist with their thumb sticking out. The seven chosen players quietly wander among the others and each one presses down the thumb of one person. (No peeking when that happens!) The chosen seven then return to the front of the area and the leader says, "Heads up, seven up!" The players whose thumbs got pressed down take turns trying to guess which of the chosen seven pressed their thumb. If they guess correctly, they switch places with that player. If they don't, the thumb-presser gets to keep his job for another round.

Fun Facts: Heads Up, Seven Up has probably been played in every elementary school classroom in America, but no one knows where it originated. Mark Twain references a game called Seven Up on at least two occasions in his writings, but that's more likely to mean a card game that was popular during Twain's lifetime.

Hide-and-Seek

(also called All Hide and Hide-and-Go-Seek)

WHO: 3 or more players

WHAT YOU NEED: good places to hide

OBJECT: Be the last person found, or if you get found, get back home before you get tagged.

The basic game involves one person, It, closing her eyes and counting to a certain number while all the other players hide. When It finishes counting, she calls "Ready or not, here I come!" and begins looking for the players. The game ends when all players have been found or tagged.

Variations

- You can count to twenty-five, fifty, one hundred, or any number you want to.

- You can create a home base (a tree, a wall, etc.) that is a "safe" territory.

- It can say, "One, two, three on Sam!" (or Lawrence, or Amy) when he finds them, then both race for home. If the hider gets there first, he yells, "One, two, three, home free!" but if It gets home first, the hider becomes It's helper and starts searching with him.

- If one person is still missing after everyone else has been found, you can yell, "Ollie, Ollie, all in free!" and that person gets to come out of hiding without being penalized.

- Flashlight: This must be played at night. It uses a flashlight to find the hiders, zapping them with a beam of light to reveal their hiding place. When a player is found, he takes the flashlight and becomes It.

- Kick the Can: Home base is a can. Everyone hides while It counts to thirty. When he spots someone, he runs back home, puts his foot on the can, and says, "One, two, three on Emily!" (or whomever), and that person must come back to home base and be a prisoner. If she realizes she's been spotted before It makes it home, she can try to beat It home and kick the can away. Then that person, and any other prisoners, are free to run away and hide again. Prisoners may also be freed by any player who can sneak up and kick the can without being caught by It. The game ends when It has taken everyone prisoner.

- Sardines: All players close their eyes and count while just one person hides; then everyone looks for that person. As each seeker finds the hidden person, she joins the hidden person in his hiding spot until the hiding spot is crammed full like a can of sardines. The game is over when the last seeker finds the hiding spot. She can be the new It or, if you prefer, everyone can race back to home base and whoever gets there first can be the new It.

Fun Facts: We know for sure that Hide-and-Seek was played in seventeenth-century England, and possibly much earlier. Like Tag, this is a game that comes naturally to children.

Hunt the Thimble

WHO: 3 or more players

WHAT YOU NEED: a thimble

OBJECT: Be the first person to find the thimble.

Choose a player to be the hider. While everyone else closes their eyes or waits in another room, the hider hides the thimble—sort of. It has to be in plain view, but it shouldn't be obvious. When the thimble is hidden, the hider invites everyone back into the room. If he likes, the hider can give clues by saying "freezing" if the seekers are way off the path, "cold" if they're not anywhere close, "warm" if they're getting close to it, "hot" when they've almost found it, or "red-hot" if they're all but touching it. Whoever finds the thimble gets to hide it the next time.

Tips

- Hide the object near something that is the same color so it will blend in and not be so conspicuous.

Variations

- You can hum softly (which means they're nowhere near it) or loudly (they're really close!) instead of saying "cold" or "hot" as clues.

- Hot Buttered Beans: You can use any object, not just a thimble, and the hider calls out "Hot buttered beans! Please come to supper" when he's ready for the players to come back in the room.

- Huckle Buckle Beanstalk: When a player spots the thimble, he says, "Huckle Buckle Beanstalk!" and sits down. The game continues until everybody has found the object.

Fun Facts: Versions of Hunt the Thimble have been played for at least three hundred years. Another of the parlor games so popular during the Victorian era, hosts loved it because it kept guests entertained and amused if supper was running late or if a few guests were late in arriving.

Johnny on the Pony

(also called Buck-Buck)

WHO: 4 or more players

WHAT YOU NEED: good legs and a spirit of adventure

OBJECT: Get on the pony and don't fall off—or down!

Divide into two teams, the Ponies and the Johnnys. The first member of the Ponies stands against a fence, wall, tree, or some other kind of support. The next member bends over, puts her arms around the first player's waist, and rests her head against that player's stomach.

The third player bends over and grabs the second player's waist, resting his head on top of her back. The last player does the same thing at the third player's waist.

The Johnnys line up some distance away (maybe twenty feet) and they yell, "Johnny on the pony, one, two, three!" as one at a time they run and jump as far forward on the "pony" as they can. The goal is to have all the Johnnys jump on the pony without it collapsing, but chaos usually occurs before that happens. A point is awarded for every rider the pony holds up, and for every player who fails to complete the jump. The teams then switch places and the process is repeated.

Tips

• The person who stands at the front of the Ponies (called a post or a pillow) should always be your strongest player.

• Your last Johnny should be your most agile jumper.

Variations

• Instead of grabbing one another around the waist, you can have players get on their hands and knees and lay their head on the back of the player in front of them, or players can put their heads through the legs of the player in front of them and hold on to their thighs.

Fun Facts: Johnny on the Pony is known primarily as a street game, meaning it was favored by city children whose playgrounds were usually the street in front of their apartments. Just the words *Johnny on the Pony* can make grown men smile. Part pileup, part Leapfrog, part goofy, part dangerous, it was a rite of passage for many eager to look good (and hang on!) in front of their peers and sweethearts.

Jump Rope

WHO: 3 or more players

WHAT YOU NEED: a piece of rope or cord that is 10–16 feet long

OBJECT: Jump over the rope as it swings under your feet and over your head.

Jump rope can be as simple as jumping up so your feet are in the air as a rope passes under you, or as complicated as multiple ropes swinging while multiple players jump in and out of the game. The more experienced you become, the more comfortable you'll be trying different speeds, techniques, and jumps. To begin with, though, just choose two players (called enders) to hold the ends of the rope so that the middle of it lies on the ground. (The top of the rope should curve enough to be at least a foot over your head when you jump up; the enders can move closer together or farther apart as necessary.) Have them swing the rope around in a circle long enough for you (the jumper or skipper) to note the rhythm and position. Jump in while the rope is in the air and hop up when it comes back down so it can pass underneath your feet. Take turns so that everyone gets a chance to jump. You can also have multiple people jump at the same time as long as the rope is long enough!

Here are the two main jumps you need to get started:

- Basic jump: Place your feet slightly apart, then, lifting both feet at the same time, jump over the rope when it swings down.

- Alternate jump (also called a speed step): Place your feet slightly apart, then lift one foot at a time off the ground. This must be done quickly, so that the rope doesn't catch on your second foot.

Once you get confident about basic jumping, you might try jumping to some rhymes. Jump rope rhymes are often silly, but they're actually quite helpful because the rhythm helps you know when to jump. Here's an example of a rhyme that's been around for centuries. You count down through all the months and days, jumping in on the month of your birthday, then jumping out on the date:

> Apples, peaches, pears, and plums,
> Tell me when your birthday comes.
> January, February, March, April . . . (keep going through December),
> First, second, third, fourth . . . (keep going through the thirty-first).

Here's another old rhyme. With this one, you jump into the rope as you start saying the alphabet. Whatever letter you're on when you trip and miss a jump is supposedly the initial of your true love's first name. Resume jumping, and whatever letter you're on the next time you mess up is the first letter of your true love's last name. No fair planning your trip-ups in advance if you already have a honey bunch!

Ice cream soda,
lemonade punch.
Spell the initials of
your honey bunch.
A, B, C, D . . . (keep going through Z, and then start again with A).

Jump rope is a fast game that takes a lot of energy, so there's not much time for small talk. Here are some code phrases jumpers and enders might use:

- Bluebells (also called rock the cradle): Swing the rope from side to side without going over the jumper's head.

- Chase the fox: All jumpers should mimic whatever the lead jumper does.

- High water: The rope doesn't touch the ground as it turns.

- Mustard and vinegar: Turn the rope at normal speed.

- Over the stars: Jumpers should jump once over the rope.

- Pepper: Turn the rope as fast as possible.

- Salt: Turn the rope slowly.

- Under the moon: Jumpers should run under the rope without jumping.

Variations

- If there's nobody else around to play with, you can jump rope by yourself; just use a shorter piece of rope, or fold the one you have in half and hold the folded end in one hand and the two loose ends in your other hand.

- Double Dutch jump rope uses two ropes instead of one. Enders hold both ropes and swing them alternately, in opposite directions, at the same time.

Fun Facts: Nobody really knows when people first made a game out of jumping rope, but we do know that it's depicted in medieval artwork. Early ropes were probably made of bamboo or vines, and in Colonial America, children sometimes used large wooden hoops instead of ropes to jump in and out of. The game is a tradition with both girls and boys (it was a boys' game originally), though girls often enjoy the rhymes now associated with jumping while boys tend to focus purely on the competition. Today, jump rope is a hugely popular competitive event; athletes are judged on footwork, strength, speed, routines, and other aspects. ESPN broadcasts the USA Jump Rope National Competition every June. Learn more about it at www.usajrf.org.

Laughing Game

WHO: 4 or more players

WHAT YOU NEED: a sense of humor and a straight face

OBJECT: Try not to laugh.

. . . .

Players sit in a circle facing one another. One player begins by saying "Ha!" without smiling or laughing. Then the player next to him, again with a straight face, says "Ha, ha!" The player next to her says, "Ha, ha, ha!" and so on around the circle. If you laugh or even smile, you are out of the game. The last player to stay in the game is the winner.

Fun Facts: This was a favorite game at parties during the reign of Queen Victoria of England.

London Bridge Is Falling Down

WHO: 4 or more players

WHAT YOU NEED: room to line up

OBJECT: Don't get caught on the bridge, then help your team win tug-of-war.

. . . .

Have everyone line up. Choose two players to form the bridge. Those two players clasp hands and hold their arms up in the air. The other players march through the bridge as they sing this song (melody on page 142):

London Bridge is falling down,
falling down, falling down.
London Bridge is falling down,
my fair lady.

On the word *lady*, the two bridge people lower their arms around whoever is passing through the bridge just then, capturing them. The bridge people keep their arms down and swing their prisoner back and forth while everyone sings:

> Take the key and lock her up,
> lock her up, lock her up.
> Take the key and lock her up,
> my fair lady.

The prisoner must then declare her preference for which side of the bridge she wants to be imprisoned in. She is released to stand behind whichever of the bridge people she prefers and the game begins again, using as many verses as needed (see below), and with each prisoner choosing sides as they go. Finally, when the last player is imprisoned and put in place, the two bridge people face each other, their respective prisoners line up behind them, grasp the waist of the person in front of them, and pull with all their might. The team that is left standing, or that pulls the other team to their side of the playing area, wins.

Additional verses:

> Build it up with iron bars . . .
> Iron bars will bend and break . . .
> Built it up with silver and gold . . .
> Gold and silver, I have none . . .

Variations

- As prisoners are caught, instead of going to jail, they can switch places with one of the current bridge people.

- You can make up your own verses, if you like. This song has had so many through the years, it's impossible to keep them all straight!

Fun Facts: There really is a London Bridge; there has been one for more than two thousand years. Over the years, many bridges have stood in that spot spanning the River Thames; the current one was built in 1973. Its predecessor was sold, dismantled, and reassembled, and now stands in Lake Havasu City, Arizona.

London Bridge

Traditional

Mother, May I?

(also called Captain, May I and Giant Steps)

WHO: 3 or more players

WHAT YOU NEED: room to play

OBJECT: Be the first player to reach Mother.

Choose someone to be Mother. She stands at one end of the play area, facing the other players, who line up next to one another at the other end of the play area. Mother randomly selects a player and says, "Aubrey, take two baby steps," or "Rachael, take three giant steps." The player must ask, "Mother, may I?" and wait for an answer before moving. If a player fails to ask permission before moving, he loses his turn. Mother doesn't have to give permission, by the way; she's free to say "Yes, you may" or "No, you may not!" She can even say "Richard, take one normal step backward" if she thinks Richard is getting a little too close for comfort, because the game ends when a player gets close enough to Mother to tag her.

Variations

- Make this game more fun by getting creative with your steps. Mother might ask players to take two gazelle leaps, four penguin slides, six wing flaps, or one frog jump.

- Instead of the leader commanding players what to do, players can take turns asking permission. For example, the first player might ask, "Mother, may I take four giant steps?" and Mother might say, "Yes, you may," or "No, you may not, but you may take one baby step."

- Have players who don't ask permission go back to the starting line instead of just losing a turn.

- Grandmother's Footsteps: Choose someone to be Grandmother (or Grandfather). That player stands with her back to the other players, who line up next to one another at the end of the play area. Players creep quietly toward Grandmother, who randomly whirls around to try to catch somebody moving. If she does, that person must go back to the starting line. Any player who successfully sneaks up on Grandmother takes her place.

- What Time Is It, Mr. Wolf?: Choose someone to be Mr. (or Ms.) Wolf. Mr. Wolf stands with his back to the other players, who line up next to one another at the end of the play area. One by one they ask, "What time is it, Mr. Wolf?" and Mr. Wolf answers randomly, "One o'clock," "Six o'clock," etc. The player who asked the question moves forward as many steps as the number mentioned in Mr. Wolf's answer. Instead of saying a time, Mr. Wolf can yell, "DINNERTIME!" Then everyone must run away as Mr. Wolf chases the players and tries to tag one before they get back to the safety of the starting line. If he tags somebody, that player becomes Mr. Wolf.

Musical Chairs

(also called Going to Jerusalem)

WHO: any number of players

WHAT YOU NEED: music (recorded or live), a chair for every player except one

OBJECT: Sit in a chair when the music stops.

Choose someone to be in charge of the music, either making it or starting and stopping it. Arrange chairs in a circle with the backs together and the seats facing out. There should be one fewer chair than players. When the music starts, players walk around the chairs. When the music stops, players sit in the nearest chair as quickly as they can. One player will be left without a seat; that person is out of the game. Remove a chair and start the music again. When the music stops, players scramble to get a seat and, once again, someone will be left standing up. Remove a chair, and play continues in the same way. The last player to remain in the game is the winner.

Variations

- If you don't have chairs, you can play Freeze Dance instead. When the music starts, everyone starts dancing. When the music stops, dancers must freeze in whatever position they're in (crazy as it may be!). Anyone who gets caught moving is out of the game. Play continues until there is only one person left dancing.

- You can also play Musical Statues. Forget the chairs and just have players march around the room to the music. When the music stops, players must freeze into a statue and not move. If they do, they're out of the game.

- Pass the Parcel is a slightly different version of this game and requires a box wrapped in many different layers. Instead of walking around the chairs, players sit in the chairs. As the music is played, players pass the box, or parcel, from one to another. Whoever is holding the parcel when the music stops gets to open one layer. A prize (a small toy or a piece of candy) or a forfeit (a card telling you to do something silly, such as "Crow like a chicken" or "Hop around the chairs on one foot") should be enclosed within each layer of wrapping. Inside the very last layer should be a more significant prize as a reward for the player who gets to finally open the actual parcel.

- You sit down for Hot Potato, too. As the music plays, people pass around a "hot potato" (in the old days, it really *was* a hot potato, but you can use anything that's convenient—a ball, a block, even a box of tissues), and when the music stops, whoever is holding the hot potato is out of the game.

Fun Facts: Musical Chairs was a popular game at parties during the Victorian Age. The hostess would play a song on her pianoforte (what a piano was called back then) while her guests sashayed around the room, then scrambled for a seat—much harder to do in a bustle or a frock coat than in jeans and a T-shirt!

Punchinello

WHO: 3 or more players

WHAT YOU NEED: a desire to be silly

OBJECT: Do what Punchinello says!

. . . .

Choose one player to be Punchinello. Everyone else sits or stands in a circle and Punchinello stands in the center as everybody says,

> What can you do, Punchinello,
> Funny Fellow?
> What can you do, Punchinello,
> Funny Clown?

Punchinello does something silly, like raise her eyebrows up and down really fast, flap her arms, or walk around like a duck. The other players copy her actions while they say,

> We can do it, too, Punchinello, Funny Fellow.
> We can do it, too, Punchinello, Funny Clown.

Then Punchinello chooses a successor. While she's making up her mind who to pick, everyone says,

> Who do you choose, Punchinello, Funny Fellow?
> Who do you choose, Punchinello, Funny Clown?

The new Punchinello takes his place in the center of the circle and the game continues until everyone has had a turn.

Fun Facts: It's probable that Punchinello was inspired by the Punch and Judy puppet characters that have been around since the eighteenth century. There are many variations on the verses, but the game itself seems to be the same whether it's played in America, France, Italy, or Australia.

Red Light, Green Light

WHO: 4 or more players

WHAT YOU NEED: good ears, room to play

OBJECT: Be the first person to tag the traffic light.

Choose a player to be the traffic light. She stands at the front end of the play area, facing the other players, who should line up next to one another at the other end (at least ten feet away, preferably more). When the traffic light turns her back on the players and says "Green light!" everyone starts moving quietly toward the traffic light, trying to get as close as possible before she whirls around and says "Red light!" When that happens, players must freeze where they are, and anyone caught moving has to go back to the starting line. Play continues until someone gets close enough to tag the traffic light. That player then gets to be the next traffic light.

Fun Facts: Almost every grown-up remembers playing Red Light, Green Light at one time or another, and almost every country in the world has some variation of this game.

Red Rover

WHO: any number of players, divided into 2 teams of equal number

WHAT YOU NEED: room to run

OBJECT: Try to break through the opposing team and claim one of their players.

Each team forms a long line, holding hands at waist level, and the teams face each other, about twenty feet apart. The teams take turns deciding which player they want, then calling out, "Red Rover, Red Rover, send Vera (or Roger, or whoever) right over!" That player leaves her team's line, decides which pair of hands she wants to aim for, then runs as fast as she can toward the other line, trying to break through the clasped hands. If she breaks through, she gets to take one of their players back to her team. If she doesn't break through, she has to become part of *their* team. If the runner and/or the people she tries to break through fall down, unless their hands come unclasped, that player is captured. When a team only has one person left, that person tries to break through the other team. If he can't do it, then the other team is the winner. If he does break through, though, he gets to take back a player and play continues.

Tips

- It's a good idea for everyone playing this game to be about the same size. Really big kids plowing into really little kids can result in someone getting hurt!

- Don't play this game on asphalt or cement, because someone might get knocked down and get a skinned knee. It's *really* fun to play Red Rover in the snow!

- Teams would love to have the biggest and strongest players from the other team come over to theirs, but those big, strong players are also the most likely to break through, so you might want to strategize how to capture them.

- Alternating bigger players and smaller ones is a good strategy, so that the strength of your human chain is fairly consistent. If too many people are breaking through your line, reposition your players.

- If you're the runner, look for the weakest link in the chain—that is, the two smallest, scrawniest people holding hands.

- Hold hands, not wrists, so no one gets hurt.

Ring Around the Rosy

WHO: 3 or more players

WHAT YOU NEED: a soft place to land

OBJECT: Have fun falling down.

Form a circle and have everyone hold hands. Moving to your left, have everyone walk around in a circle while you recite this rhyme:

> Ring around the rosy,
> pocket full of posy,
> ashes, ashes,
> we all fall down.

On the word *down*, everyone falls to the ground. Repeat as often as you want, walking right instead of left, or skipping or dancing instead of walking.

Fun Facts: This simple game has spawned quite a bit of controversy. Some experts say it's a nonsense rhyme that has been around since the 1400s; verses similar to this one are repeatedly documented in several countries, so that's a plausible theory, and singing and dancing games were very much a part of life in those days. But another theory suggests this verse was born during the Black Plague of England in 1665. The "ring around the rosy" matches the most recognizable plague symptom: a red circular rash. A common treatment was to give the victim a pouch of healing flowers and herbs ("a pocket full of posy") to wear, and, typically, when plague victims died, their bodies were cremated ("ashes, ashes"). In any case, this game has been a part of children's lives for hundreds of years.

Sack Race

WHO: any number of players

WHAT YOU NEED: burlap feed bags or really big, heavy-duty paper or plastic bags (the kind that dog food comes in) for each player, designated start and finish lines

OBJECT: Be the first person to the finish line.

Choose a leader. Everyone else claims a bag and lines up at the starting line. Players step into their bags, pulling them up over their legs as high as they will go. When the leader yells "Go!" players take off hopping toward the finish line. If players fall down, they get up and keep going. The first player to reach the finish line wins.

Variations

- Turn this into a three-legged race. Pair up, stand close together, and use a rope, bandanna, or old pair of panty hose to tie your inside legs together. Then pull the bag up over your tied-together legs, leaving one leg of each partner outside the bag. Use the hands that are next to each other to hold on to the bag and use your outside hand for balance.

Fun Facts: Sack racing has always been a popular event at county fairs, family reunions, community picnics, and carnivals, but it's believed the game started during the Revolutionary War as a form of entertainment for the soldiers.

Scavenger Hunt

WHO: 2 or more players

WHAT YOU NEED: a list of objects to find, a watch or cell phone to keep track of time, a camera or cell phone if you're doing a digital hunt or a container to hold the scavenged items if you're going for the real thing

OBJECT: Be the first person (or team) to find everything on the list.

Make up a list of objects to find. (You can do this as a group with the people who are playing, or you can have someone else, like a parent or sibling, make one for you.) Decide if you want to hunt individually or as teams, and if you want players to bring back pictures of the list items or the actual objects. If you are bringing back actual objects, all items must be taken or borrowed *with permission*. You're not allowed to purchase an item; you have to scavenge it! Set specific times for players to report back, as well as boundaries. The longer or more complicated the list, the more time players will need to acquire the items, and the wider the search area should be!

Once everyone has the list and the timing is set, the hunt is on! Start searching for the items, and remember that time is essential—whoever gets all the items first is the winner! Be creative: Sometimes you can get away with loose interpretations of what's on the list. For example, does a dead spider or a rubber spider qualify as the spider listed as Item 16? Your buddies will have to decide. Once you have everything on the list (or when time runs out), head back to your starting spot to compare what you found to the other players. Whoever finishes first or who has the most items on the list is the winner.

Here's a sample list to get you started, but it's easy to make up your own. Remember, the crazier, the better!

Scavenger Hunt List

A vacation souvenir
A man's hat
Ugly socks
A recipe
Something odd

Ten of something
A book about dogs
A concert ticket stub
A newspaper clipping
A business card

Something that glows in the dark
Something recycled
A piece of art
A food that starts with *B*

Variations

- Instead of searching for specific items, try to find things that start with each letter of the alphabet.

- Get creative with your list and include objects such as "something scary," "something purple," or "something happy." It's really fun to see what players will come up with!

- Create a theme for your scavenger hunt: Ask players to find items related to a favorite TV show or movie (for example, a picture of the Sydney Opera House, a toothbrush, or a toy boat if the movie is *Finding Nemo*), specific sports or colors, things that are Italian, things that are old, etc.

- You can give players an entire list to bring back, or just tell them one thing at a time if you want more interaction or want to make it more competitive (the first team back each time gets an extra point).

- Make players bring the items back to the home base, then return them—or ask people to donate the scavenged items and give them all to a charity after your hunt (but only if the items have some purposeful use).

Fun Facts: Scavenger hunts were really popular in the 1950s and 1960s, especially with high school and college kids. They'd go tearing around neighborhoods knocking on doors and asking for weird things, like snowshoes in July or beach balls in December.

To scavenge means to search through discarded material (junk!) for something you can use. The idea behind a scavenger hunt is to discover what kind of ridiculous or outrageous things people have lying around their houses. What's the weirdest thing *you* could contribute?

Simon Says

WHO: 3 or more players

WHAT YOU NEED: the ability to pay attention

OBJECT: Follow Simon's commands, but only when he says to.

Choose someone to be Simon. He stands in front of the play area facing the other players. Everyone else spreads out in a straight line next to one another. Simon gives a command such as, "Simon says lift your leg into the air," and demonstrates how he wants it done. All players must follow Simon's commands—as long as he prefaces it with "Simon says." If he calls out a command *without* saying "Simon says," any player who follows that command is out of the game. For example, if Simon says, "Turn around three times," everyone should just stand still, because Simon did not say "*Simon says* turn around three times." The last player left in the game becomes Simon for the next round.

Fun Facts: While we don't actually know who the Simon is who originated Simon Says, historians suspect it might have been Simon de Montfort, the Sixth Earl of Leicester, who married the sister of King Henry III. Of course his *son's* name was Simon, too, and there were undoubtedly a number of other Simons running around Europe during the Middle Ages, so let's just say this game has been around for a *very* long time.

Statue

WHO: 8 or more players

WHAT YOU NEED: an open area

OBJECT: Stay frozen.

Choose a player to be It. It takes each player by the arm, one at a time, swings her around in a circle, then releases her. The swung player must hold whatever position and/or facial expression she is in when she comes to a stop. He swings each player until all are frozen as statues, then he goes back to visit each one, trying to get them to move or laugh. The last player to remain frozen becomes It for the next game.

Variations

• Before It starts to swing a player around, he asks, "Coffee, tea, or milk?" and adjusts the speed of his swing to the player's preference. Coffee means fast, tea means medium, and milk means slow.

Tag
(also called Tig)

WHO: 3 or more players

WHAT YOU NEED: plenty of room to run

OBJECT: Catch someone if you're It; if you're not, stay out of It's way!

In its most basic form, tag is simply one player (It) chasing other players until he is able to touch, or tag, them. When he does, that player is either out of the game or might become the next It. There are an endless number of variations on this process—and if you're creative, you can come up with some of your own. Here is an overview of the most popular versions:

Variations

- Freeze Tag: When It tags a player, that person must freeze in whatever position they're in at the time—bent over, arms in the air, whatever. Frozen people can be freed when someone else (not It) tags them. The game ends when everybody is frozen. The last player frozen becomes It for the next game.

- Chain Tag: Choose a player to be the captain (the same as It). The captain chases the other players, and if he tags someone, that player has to join hands with him. From then on, they run together. Each player tagged joins the captain's team at the end of the line and the captain (and his followers!) continue trying to tag any players not yet caught. If a chain breaks, its members must join up again before any new captives can be added. A chain may encircle a player to capture her, but only the captain can make the tag. The last player tagged is the winner. If you have lots of players, choose two captains and make two teams; the team with the most players in the chain when the last player is tagged is the winner.

- Cops and Robbers (also called Jailbreak and Manhunt): Choose two players to be cops and choose an area to be the jail. Everyone else is a robber. As the cops tag ("arrest") the robbers, they haul them off to jail. Robbers can stage a jailbreak by tagging one of the prisoners as long as they don't get tagged themselves. The game ends when all the robbers are in jail.

- Fox and Geese (also called Pickadill): This game is played in sand or snow. Players draw a large circle in the sand or snow, with four lines running across the middle (the pattern looks like a pizza with eight slices). One player is chosen to be the fox, and the rest of the players are geese. Staying on the paths, the fox chases the geese; whoever he tags becomes the next fox. The center of the circle, where the four lines meet, is a safe spot.

- Moon and the Morning Stars (also called Shadow Tag): You need a sunny day for this version of tag. In this game, It is called the moon and players are called stars. The moon must stay in the shadow of a tree or a building while the stars move around in and out of the shadow. If the moon tags a star while they are in a shadow, that person becomes the new moon. Or instead of tagging the person, you can choose to tag a player's shadow.

- Puss in the Corner: This very old version of tag requires exactly five players. Four players form a big square, and the fifth player (Puss) stands in the middle of it. As the players forming the square try to change places, Puss tries to claim one of the empty corners before the intended person can get to it. Anyone left without a corner becomes the new Puss in the middle. If Puss isn't having any luck, he can yell, "All change!" whenever he likes, and everyone has to move.

- Rattlesnake Tag: Choose one player to be It. The other players line up, holding on to the waist of the player in front of them. The first person in line is called the head, and the last person in the line is the rattle. It tries to catch and hold on to the rattle's waist. If she is successful, the head of the snake then becomes It. If any player in the line lets go, he automatically becomes It. If you have more than five players, you can make two snakes, but still have only one It.

- Touch Tag (also called Band-Aid Tag and Sticky Apple Tag): Players can be tagged three times before they have to become It, but as they run, they must hold one of their hands over the place on their body where they were tagged the two previous times.

Fun Facts: The game of tag has probably been around since one sibling got to the last cookie before the other one did!

154

Tug-of-War

WHO: any number of players, divided into 2 teams of equal number

WHAT YOU NEED: a strong piece of rope about 50 feet long; a bandanna or T-shirt to tie around the halfway point on the rope; a ditch, railroad tie, puddle, sidewalk, or other dividing line between the teams

OBJECT: Be stronger than the other team.

Choose someone (or perhaps several someones!) to be a referee. Have teams line up on either end of the rope, with each player holding on to the rope with both hands. There should be at least six feet of rope between the teams, with another foot or two hanging at each end. Position teams so that the dividing line is perfectly centered between them. When teams are in place, the referee shouts "Go!" and each team tugs on the rope as hard as they can, trying to pull the opposing team over the dividing line. Players can't touch the ground for more than a brief second (to balance themselves, for example), and they can't have their elbows below their knees. Whichever team is successful is the winner.

Tips

• Your biggest, strongest person should be closest to the end of the rope.

• Never wrap the rope around any part of your body; you could hurt yourself that way.

Fun Facts: People have been playing tug-of-war for more than four thousand years. There's an abundance of ancient artwork depicting tug-of-war battles between civilizations around the world. But this power struggle wasn't always a game: Sailors in the 1800s tugged on ropes to maneuver the sails of their ships, and many armies used tug-of-war as a way to increase the strength and stamina of their solders.

Wheelbarrow Race

WHO: 5 or more players

WHAT YOU NEED: an open area, designated start and finish lines

OBJECT: Be the first team to cross the finish line.

Choose someone to be the referee. The other players get into partners. One partner gets down on her hands and knees, right behind the starting line; the other partner stands directly behind her. When the referee says "Go!" the standing partner reaches down and takes hold of her crouched partner's ankles, lifts them up, and walks forward as her partner walks forward on her hands. The first team to cross the finish line wins.

Tips

- Whichever partner is bigger or stronger should be the one on the ground.

- During the race, the pusher should hold the knees of the crawler, or barrow, in his hands and cradle the ankles in the crooks of his arm, above his elbows.

PARTNER GAMES

Coin Bowling

WHO: you and a partner

WHAT YOU NEED: a flat surface, some loose change

OBJECT: Be the first player to knock over the coin.

Balance a coin on its edge on a flat surface. (Larger coins, such as quarters, fifty-cent pieces, or silver dollars, will work best.) Take turns rolling other coins toward the one on its edge, and try to knock it over. The first player to knock down the coin is the winner.

Variations

- Set up multiple coins and see if you can knock down more than one coin at a time.

Coin Toss

WHO: you and a partner

WHAT YOU NEED: a wall, some loose change, chalk or a piece of string to make a line

OBJECT: Get your coins closest to the wall.

Mark a line ten feet from a wall. Make sure each partner has the same number and kind of coins. (For example, you might each have two quarters, five nickels, three dimes, and a penny.) Players stand behind the line and toss a coin toward the wall. The player whose coin is closest to the wall when all of the coins have been tossed is the winner.

Finger Jousting

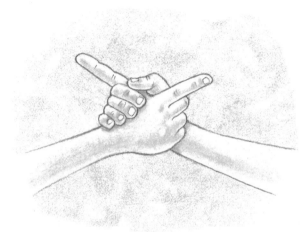

WHO: you and a partner

WHAT YOU NEED: your right arm, hand, index finger, and thumb (prejudice against left-handers is duly noted)

OBJECT: Be the first player to poke the other player.

In finger jousting, one player (called a jouster) attempts to poke (or lance) the other player with his right index finger before being poked himself. A player can poke anywhere except the lancing (right) arm.

Players can begin with a nod or a handshake, if they like. Jousters then grasp their opponent's right hand with *their* right hand, as if they were arm wrestling, and both players extend the index finger of their right hand. (Even if you're left-handed, all lancing is done with the right hand.) Jousters cannot separate their hands. If they do, whoever is at fault is penalized one point; if it happens more than twice, whichever player is at fault immediately forfeits the game to her opponent. If both players are at fault, the game is scrapped and play begins again.

You can use any sort of technique to poke your opponent, but you may not use your left hand, your arms, or your feet for anything other than dodging or stability. Officially, play time is three two-minute rounds, with one minute's rest in between rounds. Unofficially, whoever pokes first is the winner!

Fun Facts: People have been poking one another with fingers for a long time, *so it's possible* that finger jousting was a favorite sport of gladiators and the knights of the Round Table, but we don't know that for sure. What we do know is that, since the 1970s, this game has been steadily gaining popularity, and there is now a World Finger Jousting Federation to keep order and excitement in the kingdom.

Hand Games

WHO: you and a partner

WHAT YOU NEED: your hands

OBJECT: Have fun!

Do you remember playing pat-a-cake when you were really little? That's probably the first hand game most of us ever played. But there are lots more. Here are some of the best known; you and your partner can use the basic clapping pattern or make up your own.

Basic Clapping Pattern

Sit facing your partner. Both of you hold up both hands, with his palms facing yours. Clap both your hands against his, then clap your own hands together, then reach out with your right hand to clap your partner's right hand. Next, clap your hands again. Now reach out with your left hand and clap your partner's left hand. Now clap your own hands together again. Repeat clapping right hands, your own hands, then left hands, and so on. Clap in rhythm with this rhyme:

A Sailor

A sailor went to sea, sea, sea
To see what he could see, see, see
But all that he could see, see, see
Was the bottom of the deep blue sea, sea, sea.

Pease Porridge Hot

Pease porridge hot,
Pease porridge cold,
Pease porridge in the pot
Nine days old!
Some like it hot,
Some like it cold,
Some like it in the pot,
Nine days old!

Now try this clapping routine:

Pease (*clap both hands to thighs*) porridge (*clap own hands together*) hot (*clap partner's hands*),
Pease (*clap both hands to thighs*) porridge (*clap own hands together*) cold (*clap partner's hands*),
Pease (*clap both hands to thighs*) porridge (*clap own hands together*) in the (*clap right hands only with partner*) pot (*clap own hands*),
Nine (*clap left hands only with partner*) days (*clap own hands*) old (*clap partner's hands*).
(*Repeat actions for second stanza.*)

Down, Down, Baby

Down, down, baby, down, down the roller coaster. (*move your hands up and down like a roller coaster*)
Sweet, sweet baby, I'll never let you go. (*cross your arms across your chest*)
Shimmy, shimmy, cocoa bop, (*shimmy your body twice, then bop your fists on top of each other*)
Shimmy, shimmy, pow! (*shimmy your body twice, then throw your hands up in the air over your head*)
Shimmy, shimmy, cocoa bop, (*shimmy your body twice, then bop your fists on top of each other*)
Shimmy, shimmy, wow! (*shimmy your body twice, then fling your hands out on either side of you*)
Grandma, grandma, sick in bed, (*hang your head to one side and pretend to cough*)
She called the doctor and the doctor said, (*pretend to make a phone call*)
Let's get the rhythm of the head, ding-dong. (*rock your head to either side once as you say ding-dong*)
Let's get the rhythm of the head, ding-dong. (*repeat*)

Let's get the rhythm of the hands. *(clap twice)*
Let's get the rhythm of the hands. *(repeat)*
Let's get the rhythm of the feet. *(stomp one foot, then the other)*
Let's get the rhythm of the feet. *(repeat)*
Let's get the rhythm of the hot dog. *(put your hands on your hips and swing them around)*
Let's get the rhythm of the hot dog. *(repeat)*
Put it all together and what do you get?
Ding-dong! *(rock your head to either side, clap twice, then stomp twice)*
Hot dog! *(swing your hips)*
Put it all backward and what do you get?
Hot dog! *(swing your hips, stomp twice, clap twice)*
Ding-dong! *(rock your head to either side)*

Bear Hunt

Let's go on a bear hunt. *(basic clapping pattern)*
All right, let's go! *(Slap your hands on your thighs like your hands are walking)*
Oh, lookie, I see a wheat field!
Can't go over it,
Can't go under it,
Can't go around it,
Gotta go through it.
All right, let's go! *(Rub your hands together to make a swishing sound)*
Oh, lookie, I see a tree!
Can't go over it,
Can't go under it,
Can't go through it,
Let's go up it.
All right, let's go! *(Pretend to climb a tree. When you get to the top, put your hand over your eyes like you're looking around, then climb back down.)*
Oh, lookie, I see a lake!
Can't go over it,
Can't go under it,
Can't go around it,
Let's swim through it.
All right, let's go. *(Pretend to swim)*
Oh, lookie, I see a bridge!
Can't go under it,
Can't go around it,

Can't go through it,
Let's cross over it.
All right, let's go. *(Make a clicking sound with your tongue and stomp your feet)*
Oh, lookie, I see a cave—a deep, dark cave!
Can't go over it,
Can't go under it,
Can't go around it,
Let's go in it.
(Whispering) It's dark in here.
I can't see anything.
Uh-oh, I see something.
I see a big wet nose.
I see two furry ears.
I see two beady eyes.
I think it's a bear!
A bear?!?!?!
Let's go!!! *(Really fast, going backward, repeat all the sounds and adventures you just went through)*
Whew! We made it!

Little Cabin in the Woods

Little cabin in the woods, *(draw a square in the air with your fingers)*
Little man by the window stood. *(make your hands into circles, like binoculars, over your eyes)*
Saw a rabbit hopping by, *(make a fist, then hold up two fingers in the air, like a V, and bounce your hand up and down)*
Knocking at his door. *(make a knocking motion with your fist)*
"Help me! Help me! Help!" he said, *(fling hands in the air three times)*
"'Fore the hunter shoots me dead." *(put both hands together with thumbs up and index fingers pointing like a gun, and move up and down)*
"Little rabbit come inside, *(move one hand in a circular motion toward yourself as if you're beckoning someone to come to you)*
Safely you may hide." *(rock your arms like you're rocking a baby)*

The second time you repeat this rhyme, leave off the words of the first line and just do the hand motions. The third time, leave off the words of the first and second line and just do the hand motions. Continue until you are using no words, only telling the story through gestures.

Hoops and Sticks

(also called French Hoops, Flying Circles, or Graces)

WHO: you and a partner

WHAT YOU NEED: a hoop, such as a large embroidery hoop; 4 sticks (2 per player), such as dowels or skinny twigs, about 2 feet long

OBJECT: Fling the hoop back and forth and catch it on your sticks.

Players stand about ten feet apart. Each player is given 20 points at the start of the game. The first player places the hoop over both his sticks, crosses them, then as he quickly uncrosses them, he uses that momentum to fling the hoop through the air to his partner. The partner tries to catch the hoop on one or both of her sticks, then flings the hoop back in the same manner. Every missed hoop costs a player 1 point; whoever loses all 20 points first is the loser.

Variations

• Once you feel comfortable flinging and catching one hoop, try using two. You can fling both hoops at the same time, or you and your partner can both fling one simultaneously.

• If you use a larger size hoop (such as a hula hoop), instead of flinging and catching, you can roll it along the ground or sidewalk, using your stick to guide it. If you have two hoops and create a starting and finish line, you can turn your hoop-rolling into a race.

Fun Facts: Hoops and Sticks was a favorite of both boys and girls from the Victorian Age through the nineteenth century. Parents thought it taught grace and agility; kids just thought it was fun. Hoops were usually the rim of an old wagon wheel or the metal bands that went around the top of wooden barrels.

Hopscotch

WHO: you and a partner

WHAT YOU NEED: a paved or smooth surface, a piece of chalk (or masking tape), a small rock (or beanbag or other small item that won't bounce) for each player

OBJECT: Be the first player to hop all the way through the grid.

. . . .

Hopscotch is great exercise, an excellent way to improve motor skills and agility, and is a lot of fun. Use a piece of chalk to draw a basic grid of squares or rectangles (see below). Squares can be one to two feet across, depending on the age and experience of the players.

Number the squares from 1 to 9, or you can leave the last space unnumbered. Decide who will go first. That player stands facing the grid and tosses her rock (or other marker) in the first square. She hops over square 1 (never step in any square that has a marker in it!) to square 2. Then she continues hopping through the grid in numerical order on one foot. If there are two squares side by side, she lands with one foot in each square. For instance, in the image on the right, the player would jump with one foot on the 2, then to the 3 with that same foot, but then with both feet at the same time (one per square) in 4 and 5. At the top of the grid, the player jumps and turns around, staying within the last space, and hops back through the grid to square 2. From there, she bends over and picks up the marker from square 1, then jumps over square 1 and out of the grid.

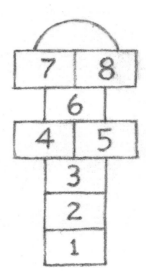

The second player can take his turn now, or the first player can play until she makes a mistake. If the second player takes his turn, he also throws his marker in square 1 and repeats what the first player did. If the first player is continuing her turn, she turns around and begins again, this time tossing her marker into square 2. Now she will hop on one foot into square 1, then hop over square 2 into square 3. On the way back, she'll stop in square 3 to pick up her marker, hop over square 2 into square 1, and then hop out of the grid. Play continues with each person tossing his marker into every square numerically and playing accordingly.

If a player makes a mistake, she leaves her marker where it is and repeats that number when it's her turn again. The other player now has to jump over the square where *her* marker is, too. Possible mistakes that end your turn include:

• you toss your marker and it goes in the wrong square.

• you hop on a space that has a marker in it.

• you step on a line (instead of inside the box).

• you lose your balance when bending over to pick up the marker and put a second hand or foot down, or fall outside the grid.

• you put two feet down in a single space.

Variations

Once you've mastered the basic game, you can get creative with your grids. Numbering and playing really doesn't change; you just use different designs to make things more fun. Two common variations are a snail grid and a snake grid, but you can probably use your imagination to come up with many more

Fun Facts: Hopscotch started out as a military training exercise for soldiers during the Roman Empire. And some football players use hopscotch as a way to improve their speed, strength, and balance.

Horseshoes

WHO: you and a partner

WHAT YOU NEED: 4 horseshoes and 2 metal stakes (at least 2 feet long), stuck in the ground 40 feet apart

OBJECT: Get your horseshoes around the ring.

Each player gets two horseshoes. Both players stand together by one stake. The first player tosses one shoe, then the other, trying to ring the stake opposite her. Then the next player throws. Together, they walk to the other stake to score. If the score is tied, whoever threw second last time throws first this time; otherwise, the person with the most points throws first. Players remain at the opposite stake and throw from there. The first player to 50 points wins.

To count, a horseshoe must be within six inches of the stake. A ringer is worth 3 points. It must circle the stake so that a straight line can be drawn from one prong to the other without touching the stake. You get 1 point for each horseshoe that is closer to the stake than your opponent's. If your and your partner's shoes are exactly the same distance from the stake, they cancel each other out.

Tips

• Hold the horseshoe with your fingers curling under the middle of the *U*, or in the middle of one of the arms. Experiment to see which of these grips feels more comfortable and how it affects your shoe's movement.

• As you toss your horseshoe, bend the knee that's on the same side as your throwing arm, and step forward with your other leg. When the shoe swings up so it's in line with your eyes and the peg, let go. Don't hurl it; let the weight of the shoe control your throw.

Fun Facts: It's believed that Horseshoes grew out of the ancient Greek sport of discus throwing. People who could not afford or didn't have access to a discus used old horseshoes instead. Horseshoes was a popular pastime for soldiers during the Civil War.

Leap Frog
(also called Hop Frog)

WHO: you and a partner

WHAT YOU NEED: room to hop

OBJECT: Just have fun!

One person bends down on his hands and knees. The other person places her hands on that person's back and uses them as leverage to leap over him. Then she crouches on the ground in front of the first player, who gets up and leaps over her. The game continues until you get tired of it.

Variations

- You can change the size of your frog (and make the leap more difficult!) by changing the position of your hands and knees:

    Easiest: Crouch as close to the floor as you can get on your knees and forearms.

    Easy: Get down on your hands and knees.

    Not so easy: While standing, bend over and grab your ankles, or rest your elbows on your knees.

    Quite a challenge: While standing, bend over and put your hands on your knees.

- Keep the Kettle Boiling: If you have more than two players, have them stand up to become a leaper just as soon as they have been jumped over. More than one person will be jumping at a time, so people must jump, then immediately bend back down.

- Sending a Letter: The first player gets into the frog position. The player who is jumping pretends to write a letter on the frog's back, bangs the stamp on the letter, then leaps over the frog saying, "Sending a letter!"

Fun Facts: Leap Frog was played in seventeenth-century England.

Marbles

WHO: you and a partner

WHAT YOU NEED: marbles; a clear section of sand, dirt, or carpet (if you're playing on carpet, you'll also need string and tape to mark a circle and starting lines on the floor)

OBJECT: Shoot your partner's marbles out of the ring.

In the basic game of marbles, you draw a ring on the ground about three feet in diameter. Each player puts an equal number of marbles (called ducks, mibs, or alleys, and measuring 5/8 inch in diameter) into the ring, either randomly or in a cross pattern. Draw two starting lines on opposite sides of the circle; the center of each line should just touch the circle. Decide who goes first by having each player send his shooter marble (also known as a taw, knuckler, aggie, moonie, or boss, and measuring 1/2 inch to 3/4 inch in diameter) from one starting line to the other. The player whose shooter is closest to the other line shoots first. Some players play for keepsies, which means you get to actually *keep* any marbles you knock out of the circle, but you can also just play for fun, called playing friendlies. Decide which way you're playing before you begin!

The first player knuckles down (read about this technique on the next page) at the starting line and shoots, trying to hit the opposing player's marbles out of the ring. In order for a player to claim a marble, it must be

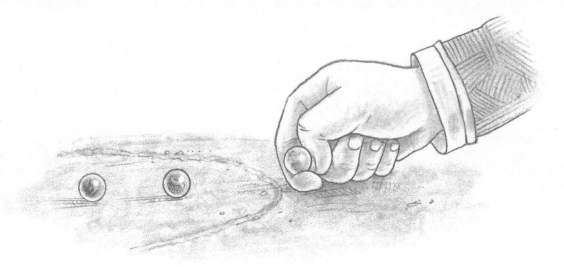

knocked completely outside of the circle—if the marble is on the line, it is still considered inside. If he does knock one out and his shooter stays in the ring, he gets to keep that marble and take another turn, knuckling down from where his shooter landed. If his shooter goes outside the ring, or if he fails to hit another marble, his turn is over. His shooter stays where it is until his next turn, at which time he shoots from that position. The game ends when all marbles have been shot out of the ring. Whoever knocks the most marbles out of the circle is the winner.

The key to playing marbles is to perfect your shooting technique, called knuckling down. Kneel on one or both knees, and tuck in your thumb and curl your fingers into a loose fist. Place your fist knuckles-down on the floor behind your shooter. Your thumb, resting on your curled index finger, should be next to the shooter. You can tilt your hand forward so that the knuckle of your index finger is just touching the ground but the rest of your hand is up, but at least one knuckle must always be touching the ground when you shoot. Now flick your thumb and send your marble flying!

Variations

- Castles: Two players kneel three feet apart, facing each other. Each builds a "castle" of four marbles, placing three in a triangle on the ground with one sitting on top. Take turns trying to knock down your opponent's castle. If you do, you get to keep all four marbles. If you miss, your opponent gets to keep your shooter. Game ends when one player runs out of marbles.

- Hits and Spans (also called Spannies): Draw a line in the dirt (or tape down a piece of string on the carpet) to be the starting line. The first player rolls a target marble from the starting line. The second player, shooting from the starting line, gets four tries to hit that marble with one of his. If he hits the marble, he gets to keep it. Any marble that doesn't hit the target but comes within a span of it (a span is the distance between the tip of your thumb and the tip of your index finger when they're spread out) goes to the first player. After the player has had his three tries, it's his turn to throw a target marble, and the other player gets the chance to hit it.

- Plum Pudding (also called Picking Plums): Each player puts a certain number of marbles on a line. Players take turns shooting and win any marbles they knock off the line.

Fun Facts: The game of marbles has been around for thousands of years; tiny stone and clay balls have been found in nearly every part of the ancient world. Children also used nuts as marbles. By the 1500s, marbles were made of glass. That's still the most popular material today.

Nine Pins Bowling

WHO: you and a partner

WHAT YOU NEED: ten 2-liter soda bottles, rinsed out; a ball

OBJECT: Knock over as many bottles as possible.

Put a few inches of water in the soda bottles to keep them from falling over too easily. Arrange the bottles in a pyramid shape on a driveway, sidewalk, or piece of flat ground. Decide which player will go first, then stand ten to twenty feet away from the pyramid, with its tip pointing at the bowler. Roll a ball toward the bottles to try to knock over as many as possible. You score 1 point for each overturned bottle. After the first player's turn, set up the bottles for the second player. The first player to 100 points wins.

Variations

• You can play to whatever number you like.

• Decorate your bottles to make the game more fun. Remove the labels and use construction paper, stickers, colored tape, or markers to make pictures or designs.

• You can also put numbers on one or more bottles, and whoever knocks them over gets to score extra points. For example, you could paint *25* on the bottle in the center of the third row, and if you knock it over, you get to add 25 points to your score.

Fun Facts: Nine pins, better known as bowling, has been a favorite American game since Colonial days. The game has actually been around since 5200 BC, and was actually part of a religious ceremony during medieval times. Dutch settlers brought bowling to America, and we've been knocking down pins ever since.

Pick-Up Sticks

(also called Jackstraws and Spellicans)

WHO: you and a partner

WHAT YOU NEED: a set of pick-up sticks or some uncooked spaghetti, wooden skewers, or skinny twigs plus crayons, markers, or paint to make your own (30 pieces)

OBJECT: Pick up the sticks without moving any others.

If you make your own set of pick-up sticks, you'll need to color them to keep track of your points. You can use crayons, markers, or paint to color the whole stick or just make a color stripe on it. Here's a list of how many sticks and which colors you'll need:

> one black stick—25 points
> seven red sticks—10 points
> seven blue sticks—5 points
> eight green sticks—2 points
> seven yellow sticks—1 point

Decide who will go first. That player stands the sticks upright, holding them in his fist. He gently lets his fist loose so the sticks fall every which way. Then he tries to pick up as many sticks as he can without letting his fingers, or the stick he's trying to pick up, move any other sticks. Once he has picked up the black stick, he can use it to help him pick up others. If he touches or moves a stick other than the one he's trying to pick up, his turn ends and it's his partner's turn to play. The player who gets 200 points first is the winner.

Fun Facts: Pick-Up Sticks has been around for thousands of years. In ancient China, pick-up sticks were made of ivory and had beautiful designs carved on them. Native Americans played this game with wheat straws.

Red Hands

(also called Hot Hands and Slaps)

WHO: you and a partner

WHAT YOU NEED: your hands

OBJECT: Slap your partner's hands.

Decide who will slap first. Players stand facing each other. The slappee hold her hands out, palms down, about chest level; the slapper holds his hands directly underneath hers, palms up. Both players take a deep breath and then the slapper whirls into action, bringing his hands out from underneath his opponent's in an effort to slap the backs of her hands with his palms. The slappee can move and dodge, and the slapper can fake a slap attack, but once the slapper has successfully slapped the slappee, his turn ends, hands change position, and the other player gets to be the Slapper.

Fun Facts: Slapping hands has been a form of greeting in America throughout the twentieth century. Though no one knows exactly how it got started, the low five—also called giving skin or slapping skin—was popular during the 1920s. One person would hold out his hand, as if getting ready to shake, and the other person would congenially slap it down. In the 1970s, a slap called the high five was born; more a celebratory gesture than a greeting, the high five calls for two people to raise a hand in the air and slap their palms together.

Rock, Paper, Scissors

(also called Rochambeau)

WHO: you and a partner

WHAT YOU NEED: your hands

OBJECT: Beat your partner's gesture.

Both players make a fist and say, "One, two, three!" as they pump their fists in the air. As they say *three*, each player commits to one of three gestures:

- Rock: A fist, so if you choose to be rock, you just leave it in a fist.

- Paper: An open hand, like you're telling someone you're five years old.

- Scissors: Your index and middle fingers extended and your other fingers curled under, like you're making a peace sign.

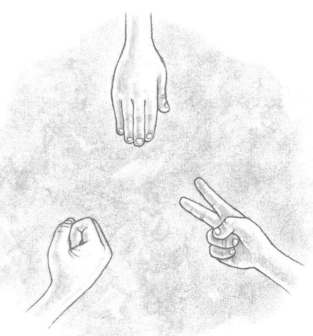

Rock beats scissors, because a rock can break or blunt scissors. Scissors beats paper, because scissors can cut paper up into little bitty pieces. Paper beats rock, because paper can cover up the rock and make it disappear. Your gesture needs to beat your opponent's; if it doesn't, he wins. If you both choose the same gesture, the game is tied and you play again. Usually, this is played as a two out of three game (whoever wins two out of three games is the winner).

Variations

• In 1994, Sam Kass and Karen Bryla (now Mrs. Kass!) invented a wild and crazy new version of this game called "Rock, Paper, Scissors, Lizard, Spock." They shared the game with friends, who passed it on, and it slowly began to show up on various Internet sites. Eventually it was even featured in a segment of TV's *The Big Bang Theory*! Sam says he and Karen invented RPSLS "because it seems like, when you know someone well enough, seventy-five to eighty percent of any rock, paper, scissors games you play with that person end up in a tie." Not only does their version of the game make a tie less likely, it also adds a ton of fun! In addition to the three standard gestures, players add Lizard (holding your hand sort of like a hand puppet, with your four fingers resting on top of your thumb) and Spock (the V-for-Vulcan finger split made famous by Mr. Spock, Leonard Nimoy's character on the original *Star Trek*). In addition to the usual rules for rock, paper, scissors above, rock crushes lizard, lizard poisons Spock, Spock smashes scissors, scissors decapitates lizard, lizard eats paper, paper disproves Spock, and Spock vaporizes rock.

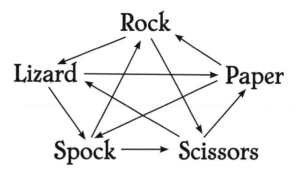

Scissors cuts Paper covers Rock crushes Lizard poisons Spock smashes Scissors decapitates Lizard eats Paper disproves Spock vaporizes Rock crushes Scissors.

Fun Facts: Rock, Paper, Scissors dates back to ancient China, around 210 BC.

Thumb Wrestling

(also called Thumb-a-War and Wiggle Waggle)

WHO: you and a partner

WHAT YOU NEED: your thumbs

OBJECT: Pin down your partner's thumb before she pins down yours.

Players hold out their hands (left or right, whichever is more comfortable) curled in a C shape and grasp their partner's hand with fingers curled into each other and thumbs lying flat on top of your fingers. Together, you say, "One, two, three, four, we declare a thumb war! Five, six, seven, eight, can you keep your thumb straight?" Then, keeping their fingers locked together, each player tries to pin down her opponent's thumb, while avoiding letting her partner pin hers. No arm movements are allowed, and the other hand cannot be used.

Variations

• Beware a "snake in the grass," that rogue index finger that tries to slither up and pin down your unwary thumb!

Tiddlywinks

WHO: you and a partner

WHAT YOU NEED: a ruler, a shallow bowl or basket, four small buttons per player (preferably 2 different colors), a larger button for the shooter

OBJECT: Get all your winks in the bowl.

Put the bowl on the floor or on a table. Place the ruler about 18 inches away from the bowl to serve as your starting line. Each player shoots one button, or wink, trying to get it in the bowl. To shoot, hold the shooter between your thumb and index finger and press down on the edge of the wink closest to you, causing it to flip in the air. Whoever gets closest to the bowl takes the next turn, shooting his wink from wherever it landed. If his wink doesn't land in the bowl, his turn ends, but if it does land in the bowl, he gets to play again with his second wink. Play continues clockwise, until one person has all four of their winks in the bowl.

Tips

• If you use an empty margarine or whipped topping container as your bowl, you can store your winks inside and use the lid to keep your game all together.

Fun Facts: The game of tiddlywinks (originally spelled Tiddledy Winks) was invented in 1889 and was originally intended for adults. Over the years, winks have been made out of ivory, bone, celluloid, wood, plastic, metal, and even vegetables! They've been round, square, and horseshoe-shaped.

Wari

WHO: you and a partner

WHAT YOU NEED: the bottom of an egg carton (remove the lid so only the 12 egg holders remain), 48 tiny pebbles

OBJECT: Get all of your partner's pebbles.

You and your partner sit down and place the egg carton between you. Place four pebbles in each of the carton's twelve holes and decide who will go first. The first player picks up four pebbles from any hole on her half of the carton, then puts one each in the next four holes, moving to the right. The second player does the same thing, choosing any hole they want. Play continues back and forth until a player's pebble lands in her opponent's side of the carton in a hole with two or three pebbles. The player whose side of the board it is claims the

pebbles and sets them aside. If the hole immediately to the left of that hole is also on that player's side and has two or three pebbles in it, he claims those pebbles as well.

If there are twelve or more pebbles in a hole a player picks from, the player picks up the pebbles and places one in each hole as he moves around the board, skipping the hole they came from originally. If the hole has any number of pebbles other than two, three, or twelve, a new pebble may be added. If your opponent's row is empty, you must try to put at least one pebble on his side. If that's not possible, or if you are out of pebbles, the game is over and the last person to move gets all the remaining pebbles in the egg carton. Whoever has the most pebbles wins.

Fun Facts: Wari is an Egyptian game more than a thousand years old. Over the centuries, Wari boards have been made from clay, stone, and wood.

ACKNOWLEDGMENTS

Thanks to . . .

Charles Nurnberg for the chance to write this book, Dawn Cusick for introducing me to Charles, and Angela Dove for introducing me to Dawn; Kate Ritchey for her good eye, good ear, and superb editing skills; Todd Dakins for bringing my words to life with his terrific artwork (the burping buffalo cracks me up!); Melissa Gerber for an awesome layout; all the folks at Imagine and Charlesbridge for their assistance and expertise; my sons—John, James, and Jaron—for telling me which games they liked best growing up and for keeping me company during late-night writing sessions; my husband, Jose, for companionable silence on weekends as we worked on our respective projects (ha! I finished first!); my cousin Heidi Johnson for "insider information" on a few games; Angie Baker for encouragement, accountability, and testing my kite directions; Aubrey Curtis for getting me excited about this book's potential; Morton Chalfy, Earl Chinn, John Disher, Roger Jaudon, Joe Lyles, and Vera Stanfield for contributing memories of childhood games; Thad Winzenz for information about the National Yo-Yo Contest; Sam Kass for sharing his fun update of a classic; and all my friends and family for their ongoing support.

INDEX

Games for One or More Players

Games for Two or More Players

Games for Three or More Players

Games for Four or More Players

Games for Five or More Players

Games for Large Groups